This can be completed by the owner, or perhaps in pencil by someone else if the book is a present!

Model:

Colour: Registration number:

Extras: When purchased:

Distinguishing marks/dents/scratches etc:

Condition: Excellent ☐ Good ☐ Fair ☐ Bad ☐ Unloved ☐ Other ☐

Most memorable experience in the BMW:

Longest journey:

Best passenger:

Worst passenger:

BMW Club membership:

Other BMW you'd most like to own:

Any other comments:

Picture:

Affix here

BMW

DRIVER'S BOOK

Foulis

Haynes
®

BMW 735

A **FOULIS** Motoring Book

First published 1990

© James Ruppert & Haynes Publishing Group 1990

Published by:
Haynes Publishing Group
Sparkford, Nr Yeovil, Somerset BA22 7JJ

Haynes Publications Inc.
861 Lawrence Drive, Newbury Park, California 91320 USA

British Library Cataloguing in Publication Data
Ruppert, James
  BMW driver's book.
  1.   Cars
  I.   Title
  629.2'222
  ISBN 0-85429-625-5

Library of Congress catalog card number 89-85905

US softback edition ISBN 0 85429 846 0

Editor: Mansur Darlington
Page layout: Chris Hull
Printed in England by: J.H. Haynes & Co. Ltd

Contents

FORE WORD

If Jesus Christ suddenly appeared in my living room and said, "Dear Ken, lay down all your worldly goods and follow me" I'd say "Gosh, I'd love to, but can't I keep my BMW?" I think he'd disapprove, even though I'd be able to follow him a lot faster in my 325i.

It's been about twenty years since I bought my first car, which I got from Jack Barclay of Barclay Square. It's probably the poshest car showroom in London's West End, brimming with Rolls-Royces and Ferraris. I must have been a great embarrassment to them, as I ordered them to get me a Fiat 850. It was a sweet little tin thing with a washing machine for an engine and I loved it dearly. But two years later, my life took a great upward turn as, flushed with cash from my wages as a Radio One DJ, I purchased my first BMW. Life suddenly became worth living. I've had nine other BMs since, and nothing on Earth would induce me to change brands.

They are, to me, the most perfect object ever made. Superb craftsmanship, brilliantly engineered, incredibly reliable and remarkably understated.

If Jesus Christ ever did decide to arrive in my living room, he'd probably arrive in a BMW!

(Photo courtesy Capital Radio).

Kenny Everett

6

*I*NTRO*D*UCTION

I'm actually responsible for several BMWs that you might see on the roads today. No, I'm not a designer, engineer, or anything useful like that, but I once held the humble rank of BMW sales executive.

For a period of my life that was all too short I ate, slept, drove and sold BMWs. As you can imagine, I was spoilt rotten. 316 one minute, 635 the next, yet I never took them for granted. They were exciting, powerful and built to perfection. All the memories are good, with one exception.

My worst moment with a BMW occurred whilst I was valuing a customer's very ancient 7 series. Everything seemed fine until I got inside. Making sure that all the toys worked I pressed an electric window button. Almost immediately and to my total horror the window dropped straight down into the door frame. I spent the next half hour trying to fish it out! Explaining how the window had acquired so many scratches wasn't easy.

I hope you enjoy reading the *BMW Driver's Book* because that's the intention. You should be able to dip into any chapter at random and find out something you didn't know about BMWs. Then of course you can go and bore someone else with it. And to make sure that you've been paying attention there's a light-hearted BMW Trivia Test. Clever dicks can start with the quiz and work backwards.

Whether you've got a brand new BM, one in four corners of your garage that you've been meaning to reassemble, or you're just saving and dreaming, there's something in the *BMW Driver's Book* for you.

James Ruppert

7

THANX...

Without other people willing to put up with your tiresome phone calls, endless letters and constant requests for photographs, a book like this would be rather thin. So here they are, the people who really deserve all the thanks.

Dee for encouragement and patience through the many midnight hours. Everyone at the BMW archive particularly George Halliday and Peter Zollner who let me rummage through their files in Munich. As well as being incredibly helpful, knowledgeable and good-humoured they always made sure I was well fed. Friedbert Holz at the Munich Press Office and Michèle Cory at BMW (GB) who both responded instantly to my requests. Steve Bliss at WCRS Mathews. Marcantonio who patiently explained why BMW advertising is so good. The BMW Car Club. John Macknay at Hartge. G. Arnold at the BMW Drivers Club. M.J. Macartney at Jaymic for telling me about 2002s. Jim Muldrew at Aitken (Builders) Ltd. Professor Gustav Foresight for compiling the trivia test. Paul Atterton at Sotheby's. Anne Bridges at Petrofina (UK) Ltd. Martin Roberts and Lindsay Ogilvy at Alpina. Jim Ballie at Fleming Thermodynamics. Mark Smith for helping me out with the used section. Betty Boop! Ivan Dutton. David Iles at Griffin Motorsport. Jon Pressnell at *Autocar & Motor* for digging out the pictures. Peter Relph. Brian Orris at the Isetta Owners Club. Rob Iles and Rod Grainger at Haynes. Also all of the authors who have written about BMWs in the past. Mum and Dad for their continued support and encouragement. And many thanks to Kenny Everett for agreeing so readily to write the amusing foreword.

And thanks to anyone else I've shamelessly left out. I hope they know who they are.

THE *BMW* HERITAGE

The first car to wear proudly the distinctive blue and white roundel of the Bayerische Motoren Werke wasn't even German. It was small, slow and British. Amazingly the original BMW was an Austin Seven!

Incorporated in 1916, BMW initially built aircraft engines under contract and then went on to design power units of its own. And as BMW came to specialize in aero engine manufacture the reasoning behind the familiar roundel designs becomes clear. The rotating blades of an aircraft engine are frozen, painted blue and white (the state colours of Bavaria) and then surrounded by the company's initials.

As well as aircraft engines, BMW diversified into manufacture of engines for many

BMW 3/15 "Dixi".

Are they by any chance related?

An Austin 7.

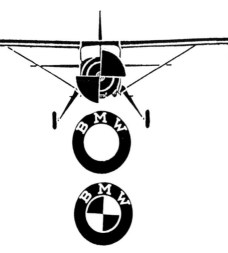

industrial and commercial uses, for which they developed a small flat-twin engine. That unit was picked up and used by a sister company to power a motorcycle. Not surprisingly BMW felt that they could do better.

cars, the development boys in Munich took the 3/15 a stage further with the faster and unbelievably cute 3/20 in 1932.

However, BMW wanted to build cars that could compete directly with the prestigious marques such as Opel and Mercedes.

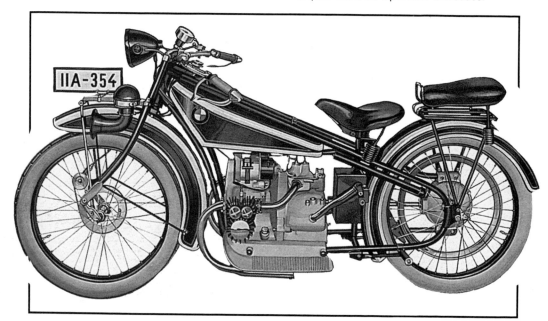

The R32 was shown for the first time at the Paris Show in 1922 and announced to the world that BMW had a huge technological lead in motorcycle manufacture. One of the most unusual features was the shaft drive that replaced the more conventional chain and is the method of delivering power to the rear wheels that is still used on today's BMW superbikes. From that point on, BMW consolidated that motorcycle reputation and went on to dominate competition throughout the '20s and '30s.

If two wheels were good, four wheels were better. When they took over the Dixi Automobil Werke on October 1st 1928, BMW also acquired the licence to build the British Austin Seven and with it a large slice of the German small car market.

As BMW began to get the hang of building

Two more cylinders were grafted on to the existing 3/20 and produced the six-cylinder 303 in 1933. To this day BMW is renowned for the smoothness and performance of its 6-cylinder units. Gone was the traditional flat grille, the 303 featured the now familiar kidney grille.

Although the 303 represented a tremendous step forward, it still lacked outright performance. The answer was to enlarge the output of the engine and introduce a new model called the 315 in 1934.

The most potent version of the 315 was the 315/1 which also set the style for all the 1930s BMWs with its steeply angled windscreen, sharply sloped tail and completely enclosed rear wheels.

The 315 designation identified it as a "3" series car with a 1.5 litre engine. This

particular method of identification was not returned to until the '70s with the 316, 318, 520, 728 etc etc . . .

The thirties marked a period of great growth and technical advancements for BMW. The 315 and 315/1 was succeeded by the 1.9 litre 319 and 319/1, which was in turn replaced by the 329 and culminated in the high performance 328 roadster which claimed an incredible number of racing victories.

Milestone models: 328

Impact

One of the quickest, most advanced and beautiful roadsters of the 30's was the 328.

Technical

The sports chassis of the earlier 315 and 319 now included box section crossmembers. The 1971 cc engine also featured an aluminium cylinder head. To stop this potent package the brake was beefed up by a hydraulic system. For competition purposes it was possible to order a ZF gearbox, larger fuel tanks and centre lock wheels. Like today's M3 the 328 was ready to race almost immediately.

Range

Although the majority of 328s were built as roadsters, five special models (2 coupés and 3 rebodied roadsters) were entered for the 1940 Mille Miglia. The closed coupés achieved speeds in excess of 130 mph and easily won the race. The war of course stopped any further development.

Legacy

A version of the 6-cylinder engine powered the British Bristol into the '50s. The highly successful Jaguar XK 120 bore a remarkable similarity to the 328. For BMW it established a sporting tradition that helped revive the marque throughout the '60s and '70s.

THE BRITISH CONNECTION

German industry became part of the war effort. However, they still managed to produce cars right up until 1941.

Other models

326, BMW's first four-door arrived in 1936. 320, a combination of the 319's suspension and 326's chassis. 321, successor to the 320. 327, made up of various BM bits, but what a beautiful result. Also offered as a convertible. 335, the biggest BMW of the time. Just 40 of these four-door convertibles were built.

When the war ended, all of BMW's manufacturing plants were either dismantled, confiscated, or, like Eisenach, on the other side of the "Iron Curtain". In fact, the East Germans were the first to restart production of BMWs in 1945. They were largely the pre-war 321s and 327s. Eventually the West won back the right to use the name BMW. But then all the East Germans did was call them EMWs, which stood for the Eisenach Motoren Werke, and paint the blue part of the roundel red!

It was not surprising that such increasingly sporty and successful cars should come to the attention of Englishman H.J. Aldington whilst competing in the Austrian Alpine Trials. He was so impressed that his company, Frazer Nash became the official importer for the British market.

From BMW building Austin Sevens under licence in Munich, a British company was now assembling right-hand drive versions of the 319! By 1939 BMW were one of the most respected manufacturers in the world, but Hitler was already making threatening moves. The invasion of Poland immediately brought BMW into the conflict and like the rest of

The British connection II

The most significant steps toward a full BMW revival started in Britain. H.J. Aldington, who held the original Frazer Nash licence, had it renewed and then turned over production for the 327 and 2.0 litre engine to Bristol Cars. Like BMW, Bristol had originally produced aircraft engines and were looking for a chance to diversify. The 1938 327 Coupé therefore formed the basis for the Bristol 400, which kept a continuity for the model identification system by being a 4th series car. That 2.0 litre engine in modified form powered all Bristols right up until 1962.

BMW's own re-entry into the car market was slow. Initially they manufactured anything that was cheap, practical and could contribute to Germany's post-war industrial revival, and that included kitchen pots, coal scuttles and metal cabinets. The first all new BMW, the 501, didn't appear until 1951.

The 501A, recognisably BMW and updating the '30s style, it was nicknamed the baroque angel. Powered by the pre-war 2 litre 6-cylinder. It wasn't fast, or cheap, but it was reliable and consequently a favourite amongst taxi drivers. Initial supplies of 501s

came in any colour you wanted so long as it was black. As you can see this pretty Baur Cabriolet didn't. However, BMW were torn between producing cars which would regain their performance reputation and cars that would satisfy the practical demands of the market place. The 1955 Frankfurt Motor Show demonstrated this conflict.

On one part of the stand were the stunningly beautiful 507 and 503 sports models, and on the other a bubble car. 503 featured a 3.2 litre V8 with light alloy bonnet and boot lids, yet was still heavier than contemporary saloons.

Milestone models: 507

Birth

In the early fifties Sales Manager Hanns Grewenig wanted to broaden the BMW range with a sports car that would utilise the available lightweight V8. The fact that Mercedes had just introduced the spectacular gullwing 300SL, aimed specifically at the American market spurred BMW into action.

Men behind it

Max Hoffman, an expatriate Austrian, probably the largest and most influential importer of cars to the USA also brought considerable influence to bear on the decision to go ahead with the project. He not only spotted the gap in the market for such a car, but also persuaded Albrecht Goertz to submit his designs to Munich.

Impact

It took just 18 months to get these cars onto the production line, but deliveries were slow and the price steadily increased. Although the body was beautiful and the performance electrifying, just 253 examples were sold.

Legacy

Although the 507 might not have made the commercial grade, it did prove that BMW could once again produce sports cars of the highest quality. But the world wasn't ready for it.

Profile: Albrecht von Goertz

Significance

If you asked most people what they thought was the most beautiful BMW, the immediate answer would be, the 507, and the man who designed this '50s classic is quite remarkable.

Early years

His proper title is Count Albrecht von Goertz whose ancestral home is a 13th century house near Hanover. But in spite of his background, Goertz was a 'free spirit', travelling first to England, then America, where he worked on the West Coast. In fact, he was one of the original customisers, building hot rods and all sorts of special cars.

Designs

However, it was only after service in the US army during the war that he got his first real job in the motor industry as an apprentice stylist with Studebaker. By 1952 Goertz was accomplished enough to set up his own studio in New York.

Legendary events

In 1954 he offered his services to BMW and they accepted. The brief was to capture the spirit of the earlier 328 roadsters and provide an answer for the Mercedes 300SL gullwing.

Visually the 507 was an unqualified success, if commercially it didn't have the desired impact.

He has been involved in many other projects from furniture to clothes, although another classic car design did flow from his pen many years later in the form of the Datsun 240Z.

Postscript

Goertz is still retained by Munich as a consultant on styling matters, which means that his brilliant influence is still felt in today's designs.

By contrast, the Italian Isetta Bubble car was powered by a 250, or 350 cc motorcycle engine and built under licence. They proved to be very successful and a common sight on the roads of Britain, not least because of the low taxation levels on three-wheeled cars and the frugal fuel consumption.

If you thought that the Isetta bubble was the only BM not to sport kidneys, here's one fitted with knee ventilation grilles.

The British connection III

In 1957 Ronnie Ashley, an ex-BOAC Captain, formed a company called Isetta of GB to build BMW bubble cars in a former locomotive erector's in Brighton. The parts arrived by train and later left the factory fully assembled by the same route.

However, by 1960 BMW were in financial dire straits and to develop new models, re-structuring was essential. Bavarian financiers made sure that this was done.

BMW then decided to stretch the Isetta from a bubble to a droplet which was called the 600. Unfortunately it did not prove to be popular, even though you could get two suitcases and the wife inside without excess baggage on the roof.

BMW's next step was to design something that looked much more like a car even though it used their own flat-twin motorcycle engine. As this publicity shot clearly shows there's now room for four grown-ups and the faithful mutt. In both coupé and saloon guise the 700 proved to be BMW's most popular post-war car to date. Between 1959 and 1965 over 180,000 were sold.

Early years

Profile: Herbert Quandt

Significance

If it wasn't for Herbert Quandt and his half brother Harald, there probably wouldn't be the BMW that we all know and love today!

Herbert's father had built up a large and successful company and the two brothers joined him after the war, becoming equally accomplished speculators. Herbert in particular became known as risk taker and gambler despite being quite shy and cagey about his business activities.

Saviour

By 1960 both brothers had set their sights on BMW. They carefully acquired some two thirds of the shareholding, with Herbert holding the largest amount (40%). Now that they were in control they set about reorganising its structure, appointing trusted representatives and motor industry experts rather than taking up their positions on the board. With the Quandt banking fortune behind it BMW could invest in and develop the *Neue Klasse* saloon. The rest, as has often been said, is history.

Postscript

The Quandt group still retain control of BMW although Herbert resigned his seat on the board when he was seventy and died just two years later in 1982.

What BMW aimed to do was build prestigious cars that would satisfy the demands of the ever more affluent West German consumer. There was almost no development period for this *Neue Klasse* (New Class) of car, as BMW had to produce something at the 1961 Frankfurt Motor Show in order to generate business. An all-new, but well developed 1500 cc engine provided the power, whilst MacPherson front suspension with semi-trailing arms at the rear provided a superlative ride. The Neue Klasse was ready. Nearly thirty years later the 1500 is still instantly recognisable as a BM.

Milestone models: 1500

Birth

When BMW were rescued from bankruptcy in 1960, they got a valuable breathing space which allowed them to design a new family saloon from scratch. That clean sheet of paper produced BMW's most important model in its history. However, they needed to get the car to the marketplace as soon as possible, so Italian design firm Micholetti quickly grafted a kidney grille on to the hastily developed body.

Impact

The prototype at the Frankfurt Show in 1961 caused a sensation. Simply called the 1500 it was clearly one of the most advanced saloons in the world and easily lived up to the "New Class" tag that BMW had given it.

Here a young lady seriously damages the re-sale value, and possibly bonnet, of a Bertone 3200CS prototype.

Technical

Power was provided by a modified four-cylinder that was originally intended for the 700 models. Styling was boxy but crisp and provided excellent interior accommodation. Handling was assured and advanced, being the first production car to utilise MacPherson Strut front suspension.

Legacy

Although production was initially slow, the 1500 proved to be a commercial success and formed the virtual blueprint for every BMW that has followed. In fact, it is possible to establish a direct link from the 1500's engine to BMW's World Championship win in '83. Motorsport engineers found that the best basis for the turbocharged unit was a well used 1500 cc block!

Another quite different model also signified the new BMW era. The Bertone-designed 3200 CS Coupé introduced in 1962 retained the V8, the last BMW to do so, and also set the "style" for all the coupés that followed.

The new class family

The 1500 was used by BMW as their main platform for further model development. This meant that many components would be shared and a clear marque identity would be apparent across the range.

1963: the 1800 was introduced, with an 1800 cc engine and chrome bodystrip to distinguish it from the smaller model. It was followed by a high performance TI (Touring Internationale) version.

1966: 2000 Used coupé engine and rapidly became the most popular BMW. In its first year, over 43,000 were delivered to eager customers. Not surprisingly a TI version followed, and later the first fuel-injected BMW, the 2000tii.

Milestone models: 2002

Impact

BMW can lay claim to inventing several categories of car and with the 2002 the small sports saloon was born. The 02 series had already opened up a new and much younger market for BMWs.

Range

The twin carbed 2002ti had 120 bhp and a 115 mph top speed. The Touring variant pre-empted the hot hatchback trend by quite a few years and of course the principle has since been revived for 1988's 325i Touring.

Legacy

The 02 models evolved into the 3 series which is now BMW's most successful and profit-making model. Progress for the company into the '90s still depends on it.

The first hot hatchback in most potent form, 2002 tii Touring.

2002 Turbo – the fastest of
the lot – 130 mph!

1966: The 02s. BMW, keen
to broaden the appeal of
the existing range by
offering more bodystyles,
introduced the 1600–02, a
two-door that was lighter
and consequently fast.

Glaserati

For a short time 1967–9 BMW returned to selling V8 sports cars. This occurred because they acquired a bankrupt sports car manufacturer called Glas. The cars were designed by Frua of Italy and nicknamed Glaseratis because of their resemblance to contemporary Maseratis. Although they wore the distinctive blue and white roundel of BMW, the kidney grille was not incorporated. More importantly though, the Glas factory in Dingolfing offered room for BMW to expand and that's exactly what they did from the late sixties to seventies. Today Dingolfing is the main manufacturing plant for all BMW models.

Six appeal

This is the archetypal six-cylinder BMW: the 3.0Si, with an archetypal Bavarian maiden. For many, a real BMW must have a six-cylinder engine. The versatile 1500 unit lent itself ideally to this development and in 1968, the new 2500 and 2800 saloons were announced. These proved to be very popular being both fast and practical and the 2500 in particular stayed in production, almost unchanged for nine more years.

The first '6' coupé 2800CS which featured a new front end design similar to the saloons. The Coupés were rapidly developed over the succeeding years, mainly for the purposes of motor sport, but this also produced some very exciting road cars. The 3.0 CSL (Coupé Sport Lightweight) versions had alloy skins on the doors, boot and bonnet to reduce weight and made them incredibly quick – 138 mph and 0–60 mph in 6.8 seconds.

In 1972, BMW not only showed off its unique "4-cylinder" Munich headquarters which coincided with the Olympic Games, they also replaced the 2000 with a new mid-sized saloon, the 5-series. The all new body retained the suspension set-up and four-cylinder unit of the earlier car. It didn't receive six cylinders until 1977, but thereafter 2.5, 2.8 and 3.5 litre versions were offered. BMW returned to identifying its cars by model and capacity. The was a 5 series car with a 2.0 litre engine, hence the 520. Geddit????

BMW made sure of mass market appeal when in 1975 the 3 series cars arrived to take over from the much loved 02s. These were much heavier cars than their predecessors, but the small six-cylinder engines soon

improved the power-to-weight ratio and performance figures to produce exciting models like the 323i.

At the luxury end, the Coupés were developed into the more refined 6 series in 1976. Here a 633 competes with a fur coat to warm the cockles of the model's heart.

The arrival of the 7 series saloon in 1977 demonstrated that BMW could match anything offered by either Mercedes, or Jaguar. Consistently the 7 has incorporated technological advances ahead of the rest, such as Anti Lock Braking (ABS) and digital electronics.

Entering the eighties with such a complete and successful model range meant that BMW were in a position to make even greater advances. But that's another story: see 'BMW today!'

27

BMW IN COMPETITION

BMW and motorsport are almost inseparable. As a company they have always recognised that competition success soon translates into waiting lists for their equally potent road going cars.

Their first competition victories were achieved on two wheels with that famous flat-twin engine. Between the start of motorcycle manufacture in 1922 and 1925, BMW scored over 100 race wins.

With the Dixi, BMW acquired a car with an impressive racing pedigree, both in Germany and in England as the Austin Seven, winning numerous hill climbs and rallies. Not sur-

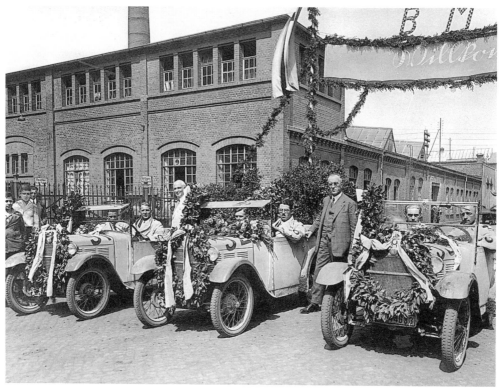

prisingly BMW made sure that in their hands the Dixi would go on to many more victories. Three BMW 3/15s as they were now called, scored an impressive team victory in the 1929 Alpine Rally and later a class win the 1931 Monte Carlo Rally. As you can see, the boys look ecstatic after winning the Alpine at an average speed of 26 mph.

It was the six-cylinder cars that really earned BMW their racing spurs. In 1934 the 315/1 emulated the rally successes of the smaller car in the Alpine and Monte Carlo events. And in its Frazer Nash guise, the 315/1 scored many victories in Britain and Europe. The 2 litre 328 that arrived on the race tracks in 1936 with uprated engine, independent front suspension and precise rack and pinion steering heralded a completely new era. They produced class wins in endurance races such as the 1938 Spa-Francorchamps and 1939 Le Mans. In fact, the victories were so numerous that even the official BMW history doesn't list them all.

This is the start of a 2 litre race in 1938. As you can see, several 320s are taking part. And if you're interested No.10 was the winner.

The British connection IV

After the war, whilst the factory concerned itself with getting road cars into production, it was left to privateers and the British to race for glory! In fact, the majority of cars used for competition in this period had an engine that was based on the 6-cylinder BMW unit and supplied by Bristol Cars. These engines went on to power the single seat Coopers and ERAs which established Britain as an international force in motor racing.

In 1956, when motor sports events were allowed to resume in Germany, it was the baby Isettas which proved to be successful. The little 600 even won the Alpine Rally outright in 1959. But it was the 700 that received full factory backing and finally returned the company to motor racing. In its first year 1960, the 700 won outright the National Hillclimb Championship and proved itself, particularly against more powerful competition, as a nimble and powerful car. 1961 saw the 700 take the national Saloon

The most advanced 328s with streamlined Italian Touring bodies won their class at Le Mans in 1939 and several other long distances races, including the Mille Miglia, before the hostilities intervened.

Car Championship and confirm the little car's supremacy. This was valuable experience for the BMW competitions department (which had a limited preparation area in the factory), particularly as the 700 went on winning right up until 1965.

With the New Class saloons came new racing opportunities with real cars. It was the twin-carburettor 1800ti that provided

A 700 RS competes at a 1961 hillclimb event, receiving attention from a man in lederhosen, which is now forbidden under international racing rules.

2002 indulging in wheel lifting track activities and was also successful in rallies.

victories in Budapest and a class win in Nurburgring and winning the National saloon car title in its 1964 debut year. The uprated 1800TI/SA followed in 1965, being lighter, with wider wheels, increased 165 bhp, five-speed gearbox and anti-roll bars to improve handling.

The 2000TI was introduced in 1966 and took over competition duties and in 1968 scored a class win in the Monte Carlo Rally. The next generation of saloons to do battle on the race track in 1968 with the 2002s, which resulted in a European Championship and Driver's titles for that season.

In spite of continued success, the factory handed over its touring car interests to performance specialists Alpina who already campaigned 1602 and 2002s. BMW then went even further and announced that they would withdraw from racing altogether. This meant that their ambitious plans for Formula 2 which had led to the development of an engine was shelved. Even so privately entered BMWs still continued to win races both at saloon car and Formula 2 levels.

Two years after withdrawal the board reversed the earlier decision. A separate company BMW Motorsport was set up within the Munich factory.

Profile: Jochen Neerpasch

Significance

Perhaps one of the most important appointments in the history of BMW was Jochen Neerpasch in the spring of 1972 to manage the Motorsport department.

Early Years

Neerpasch had begun his racing career at Porsche as a race mechanic, but in his spare time he entered competitions in a Borgward Isabella. Moving on to Ford he eventually became a member of the Shelby-Cobra racing team in 1964.

Driver

Neerpasch drove the GT40 in the Manufacturers' Championship and when he returned to Porsche piloted the 907 and 908s.

Manager

However, in 1968 he returned to Ford and set up a competitions department and campaigned the seemingly invincible V6 Capris around Europe. That is of course until Robert Lutz, Sales Director at BMW put him in charge of Motorsport. After that it was the CSLs which became invincible!

Ambitious

Success in both Saloon and Formula 2 racing though, did not mean that Neerpasch would be allowed to contest the Formula 1 Championship. That's why he was instrumental in developing the M1 for the PROCAR series. But ultimately he had to leave. So he followed his ambitions and the turbocharged BMW four-cylinder to Talbot.

Legacy

What Neerpasch left behind was a highly organised competitions department and a revitalised BMW that had regained its racing pedigree.

The British connection V

At single seat level, an agreement was reached with March Engineering, an English company. The co-operation meant that BMW would provide its M12/6 2 litre engine for the March 732. This combination proved to be almost unbeatable. Their first Formula 2 season in 1973 saw the French driver, Jean-Pierre Jarrier take the Championship outright. This success was repeated in 1974, '75, '78, '79 and '82.

As the for saloons, BMW now had the large powerful 6-cylinder coupés with which to do battle on the race tracks of Europe, whilst the specialist teams, such as Alpina and Schintzer also fielded their own 3.0 CSLs. It was the 1973 season which saw BMW take on their Ford rivals head on. The turning point for the works cars was the adoption of the now familiar wings, spoilers and air dams which gave them incredible stability. This led to a crushing defeat of the works Ford Capris. Ironically most of the Motorsport team of engineers and drivers had been racing with Ford the previous season! BMW went on to overall victory in the European Touring Car Championship for that year.

An equally prestigious success in 1973 was the CSLs' first major international victory which was an outright class win at Le Mans.

In 1974 both Ford and BMW equipped their cars with new and more powerful engines, keeping the excitement levels high and the Touring Car Championship in German hands.

Championship-winning BMW-March 742s with Champ Patrick Depailler on the left and runner-up Stuck on the right. Not surprisingly, everyone else is trailing in their wake.

A CSL giving a couple of Ford Capris a hard time.

33

BMW driver: Hans Stuck

Hans Stuck Senior was one of BMW's most famous driver's becoming Hillclimb Champion 1960 at the wheel of a 700. Not surprisingly his son managed to follow very successfully in his footsteps. Much of the credit for the '70s CSL success can be attributed to Stuck. These days he's one of P*****E's best works drivers. Perhaps he'll return to BMW if they step up their racing programme.

CSL hotly pursued by P****s.**

Aware that the BMW name needed to be re-established in that lucrative North American marketplace, the Board acquired the American concession and then made a determined move on to the race tracks. It was the CSLs which contested races all over America and although they were successful, particularly against the Porsche 930s, they didn't win the Championship outright.

The next year BMW switched to the turbocharged 3 series producing the 320i version in 1977. In the hands of British driver David Hobbs it won four stateside races.

In Europe the Formula 2 engine was used to power 320is in a so-called "Junior Team" which was designed to give young racing drivers their "chance". The juniors: who would have believed that these fresh-faced lads would cause a considerable amount of circuit argy-bargy which resulted in thrills, spills and dents?

34

Here's the proof, a BMW
Junior Team sandwich!

BMW driver: Ronnie Peterson

Regarded as one of the best all-round racing
drivers and when in charge of a CSL his
performance was nothing short of exhilarat-
ing. Unfortunately his early death at the 1978
Italian Grand Prix has deprived the sporting
world of a great competitive character.

35

The **PRO**CAR saga A-

A. Schnitzer won the National title with a 1.4 litre 320 turbo in 1978.

B. While BMW had mixed fortunes with the turbocharger. A CSL turbo was developed, but proved to be almost too powerful.

C. With a top speed of 185 mph, it could leave the opposition standing, yet was unreliable enough for the opposition to leave *it* standing.

D. BMW identified their model's shortcomings particularly when compared with the lightweight, rear-engined Porsches.

E. In 1972 during the opening of the new company museum and four-cylinder building, they unveiled an arresting concept car.

F. A turbo powered, gull-winged, mid-engined supercar. . .

G. . . . inevitably started rumours that BMW were about to put such a vehicle into production . . .

H. . . . but BMW didn't really need such a model and in fact . . .

I. . . . nothing further was done with the project until 1976.

J. To homologate a new car for Group 4 racing in the Manufacturers' Championship BMW would need to build at least 400 units within a 12 month period.

K. As a result, the decision was made to offer a normal road-going version.

L. The E26 project was re-named the M1.

M. However, Motorsport could not produce the required number of cars, because of their limited facilities.

N. So renowned stylist Giugiaro and his Ital Design firm were put in charge of design and production of the fibreglass bodies.

O. From there the chassis and engine assembly would be in the hands of Lamborghini.

P. Their contract called for a production rate of two per week and a total run of 800 cars, but none of these targets were ever reached.

Q. Because of persistent delays, the bodies were shipped direct to BMW's coachbuilders, Baur who fitted the chassis.

R. Final assembly was carried out by Motorsport.

S. It wasn't until 1981 that the 400 M1's had actually been produced.

T. In the meantime BMW made sure that they got some racing use out of their expensive new super sports cars.

U. During the '79 and '80 seasons most of the World's top drivers took part in the best rewarded and fastest single-make racing championship ever.

V. The PROCAR series pitted Formula 1 drivers against privateers who all drove identically prepared M1s.

W. An M1 driven by Piquet and Hans Stuck did come third in the 1980 Nürburgring 1000 km.

Y. It had arrived too late and never really met the competition it had been designed for.

Z. However, the racing programme did at least produce one of BMW's most exciting road cars, without the wings, without adverts, but with the performance, the road-going M1.

An M1 going for an expensive spin.

Formula 1 – The British connection VI

The 16-valve turbocharged four-cylinder provided Motorsport with their next racing opportunities. In 1979 they seriously began to consider that unit for Formula 1 use. After preliminary discussions with both McLaren and Ligier the British Brabham team agreed to try the engines.

Flashback! British connection VII

Factory men Hahne and von Falkenhausen went to GB to buy a chassis for engine test purposes. What they came up with was an obsolete Brabham Formula 1 frame. And once the BMW engine was installed they ran it on nitromethane fuel for some successful world record attempts: Standing $1/4$ mile 84 mph/500 metres 88 mph/111 mph kilometre.

Disappointment

Initially the engine proved powerful but unreliable and further development work needed to be carried out. From failing to qualify in the 1982 Watkins Glen round of the World Championship, the BMW-powered Brabham went on to win the Canadian Grand Prix just two weeks later. But it was during the close season that the full potential of the Brabham and BMW combination was realised.

A BMW-powered Brabham from 1966.

M1

In 1980 he began his relationship with BMW when he and Brabham team-mate Nikki Lauda finished as M1 PROCAR Champions. And with Hans Stuck he scored the M1's best sports car result when they finished 3rd in the Nürburgring 1000 km.

Champion

Things went right for the Brabham team in 1981 and Piquet became the World Champion. Switching to BMW M Power, Brabham and Piquet became the first turbo powered World Champions. Arguably, this was BMW's and Piquet's finest racing moment.

The championship season

By the opening round of the 1983 Championship the engine had been fully modified and installed in a new body made of carbon fibre and aluminium. It was called the BT-52 and in Nelson Piquet's skilful hands it won the Brazilian Grand Prix. From there it was on to second places at the French, Monaco and British Grand Prix. Team-mate Patrese took third in the German Grand Prix before Piquet regained form to finish third in Austria and then go on to win the Monza and European Grand Prix.

Drivers: Nelson Piquet

Early years

Nelson Souto Maior won the 1972 Brazilian Kart Championship, although we know him better as Nelson Piquet. He changed his name from Maior so that his parents didn't know what he was up to!

Europe

He became Brazilian Super Vee Champion in 1976 and then set his sights on Europe. In '77 he was third in the European Formula Three Championship and in '78 won the British Championship. It wasn't long before Formula One teams were offering him drives, firstly with Ensign, then McLaren and finally Brabham, where he stayed.

Success

It then all hinged on the final round at Kyalami in South Africa, with Renault's Alain Prost just two points ahead. A third place was enough to give Piquet victory in the drivers' championship and BMW perhaps their most significant racing victory ever.

Inset: **Piquet leads Prost, the way it was to stay.**

Powered by BMW

Here's a few other sports cars that have benefited from M Power.

Würth-Arrows BMW A7 driven here by Marc Surer.

Gerhard Berger in the Benetton BMW B186.

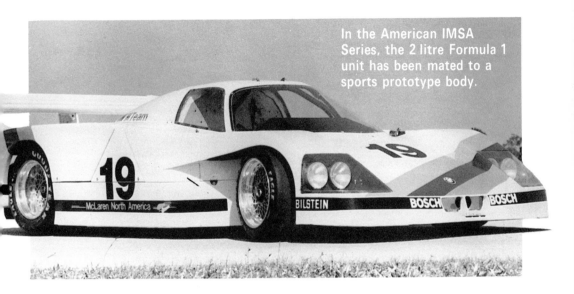

In the American IMSA Series, the 2 litre Formula 1 unit has been mated to a sports prototype body.

BMW drivers: Dieter Quester

This athletic Austrian is BMW's longest serving and most successful saloon racer of all. His first contact with the marque was on the water when he won the European Motor Boat Championship three times.

On land he has won the European Touring Car Championship four times in 2002s, a Coupé and 635. He's also had many other outings in hillclimb and Formula 2 BMWs which demonstrates his considerable versatility.

The M3 success story

No other BMW has been so successful in such a short period of time. In its first season the Championship wins were impressive.

World Touring Car Championship
European Touring Car Championship
European Hill Climbing Championship –
Racing Cars
European Hill Climbing Championship –
Group A
German Touring Car Championship

Australian Touring Car Championship
French Touring Car Championship
Finnish Touring Car Championship
Dutch Touring Car Championship
Portuguese Touring Car Championship

41

BMW Drivers: Roberto Ravaglia

This Italian driver initially found success in Formula 3 having progressed from Kart racing. But it was with the 635CSi that he first tasted lasting success, winning the European Touring Car Championship in 1986. For 1987 he took BMW's new M3 to the World Touring Car Championship.

Ravaglia represents the future for BMW and looks set to continue his excellent record of success.

M3 Road and Race

What's the difference between an M3 on the track and on the road?

Roll cage.

Perfect weight distribution 50/50.

Weight reduction to an optimum 960 kg as against 1200 kg

Racing engine – modified Motronics.

Racing transmission – short or long ratios.

Modified spring struts with adjustable spring plates.

Reinforced semi-trailing arms.

Four piston caliper disc brakes and hydraulically operated (hand) brake

Single nut release wheels.

Safety fuel tank.

No power steering.

PERFORMANCE BMWS

BMW's reputation for making cars that were both stylish and fast was established in the 1930s, totally lost after the war and not fully regained, in spite of the 700's efforts, until the 1970s.

Put numbers on the doors, enter a race and in 1972 a 2002 Turbo would probably see off any other sports car. In short, the Turbo was a racing car in production saloon clothing, something that BMW have become rather good at.

Wilheim Noll tries to recapture the speed, but certainly not style of the marque. This motorcycle in disguise actually reached 280 km in 1954. Well done Wilheim!

This is the view that many autobahn slow coaches became familiar with before the Turbo blasted past. Notice the reverse type that would actually appear the right way round in the rear view mirror. However, customers didn't like advertising the fact that they were driving a Turbo ambulance, so the graphics were changed.

The purposeful cockpit of the Turbo with the boost gauge that is now a familiar addition to many of today's cars. Back in 1972 it was unique. The first turbo available to the public. And at the moment it is BMW's last mass production turbo.

Now you know who to blame for the spoilers, skirts and other paraphernalia but at the time the 3.0 CSL was the first to have them. Those plastic bits and bobs did actually keep it on the ground once it clocked 140!!

BMW always got those wings and things in the right places thanks to the wind tunnel. Here a racing 320 feels the benefit. Notice that the badge has been removed to save weight!

If you wondered where the hot hatchback came from, here it is. The 2002 in its most potent tii form with three-door touring bodywork. Expect close to 120 mph from this one.

46

BMW Motorsport

Origins

A company within a company formed in 1972 to develop race-winning cars.

Growth

In order to meet homologation regulations for production car racing a number of models have to be built. So Motorsport effectively became a manufacturer within a manufacturer, producing totally unique race-ready competition cars.

Products

M1 The first all Motorsport car was the appropriately titled M1.

M635 CSi: Motorsport prove that the coupé can handle the extra power. This one is demonstrating its high speed paddling capability.

The Q car era begins, although the deep spoiler, and the fact that it will hurtle past you at 140 mph, gives the game away.

M5 with the 16 valve M1 engine, even more of a Q car than the original 535. 153 mph top speed!

M3 The ultimate 3 series with the four-cylinder Formula 1 engine which means 146 mph on the road.

Earning the M.

Only when a car achieves the highest standards of performance will it get the famous M. As their advertising slogan runs, "M the most powerful letter in the world."

Motorsport spotting

These are the tell-tale signs of something even more potent lurking underneath that beautiful BMW body. (a) The M badge (b) Lift the bonnet and you'll probably find an engine that's bigger than usual. Here a 3.5 litre engine in the spoilered surroundings of a 5 series means it's an M535.

The alternative BMWs

For those who still don't find their BMW fast or exciting enough a number of specialist companies exist to cater for that demand.

Alpina

One of the most famous remanufacturers of BMWs with BMW's blessing. Burkard Bovensiepen, a typewriter manufacturer, diversified into producing BMW tuning kits in the early '60s. From there full scale competition entries and racing success followed.

These exclusive cars are built in England by Sytner of Nottingham.

Base car for the start of the Alpina range is the 325i.

"ALPINA" (Alpina style without performance)
Colour coded front and rear spoilers, 7" Alpina alloys with low profile tyres, Alpina badges, steering wheel, gear and key fob.

Alpina Sport Pack

Alpina camshaft, engine management system, exhaust manifold. 190 bhp. 0–62 mph 7.2 seconds.

Alpina C2 2.7

Engine:	2693 cc with mahle pistons, alloy cylinder head, Bosch Motronic II, Alpina manifold and exhaust.
Suspension:	
Front:	progressive rate coil springs, Bilstein telescopic gas dampers
Rear:	minibloc springs, Bilstein telescopic gas dampers.
Wheels/Tyres:	2 x 7" Alpina alloys, low profile 205/50 or 225/45 VR 16 Michelin MXV
Interior:	As "Alpina" plus numbered plaque.

Alpina B11 6 Series

Engine:	3430 cc seven bearing with mahle pistons, alloy cylinder head, forced lubrication circulation, oil cooler, temperature controlled visco-fan Bosch Motronic II.
Transmission:	Five-speed manual, or EH switchable auto with special 3.73 final drive.
Suspension: F/R	progressive rate coil springs, Bilstein telescopic gas dampers.
Wheels/Tyres:	8 1/2 x 17 Alpina alloys, low profile 235/45 ZR17 Michelin MXX
Interior:	Alpina steering wheel, key fob, gear knob and badges.
Performance:	Top Speed 154 mph

Alpina B11 7 Series

Engine:	3430 cc seven bearing with mahle pistons, alloy cylinder head, forced lubrication circulation, oil cooler, temperature controlled visco-fan Bosch Motronic II.
Transmission:	Five-speed manual, or EH switchable auto with special 3.73 final drive.

Suspension: F/R	Bilstein gas filled shock absorbers with Alpina suspension springs.
Wheels/Tyres: FR	$8^{1}/_{2}$ J x 17 H2 Alpina alloys, low profile Michelin MXX 235/55 ZR 17 – 10J x 17 H2 Michelin MXX 265/40 ZR 17
Exterior/Interior:	Colour keyed front spoiler and mirrors, Alpina steering wheel, badged, key fob and plaque.
Performance:	0–62 mph 7.5 seconds. Top Speed 154 mph

Alpina B10 5 Series

Engine:	3430 cc seven bearing with mahle pistons, alloy cylinder head, forced lubrication circulation, oil cooled, temperature controlled visco-fan Bosch Motronic II.
Transmission:	Five-speed manual, or EH switchable auto with special 3.73 final drive.
Suspension: F/R	Bilstein gas filled shock absorbers with Alpina suspension springs.
Wheels/Tyres: F/R	$8^{1}/_{2}$ J x 17 H2 Alpina alloys, low profile Michelin MXX 235/45 ZR 17 – $9^{1}/_{2}$ J x 17 H2 Michelin MXX 265/40 ZR 17
Exterior/Interior:	Colour keyed front spoiler and mirrors, Alpina steering wheel, badges, key fob and plaque.
Performance:	0–62 mph 7.5 seconds. Top Speed 156 mph.

Hartge Motorsport was founded by Rolf and Herbert Hartge in the early '70s to provide the widest possible and most compatible modifications for BMWs. To this end they are actually recognised as a motor manufacturer. This work is carried out in Britain by Birds Garage. Hartge conversions are unique in that they are modular and allow the BMW to be built to the customer's exact requirements. Here's a selection of the complete Hartge modified cars.

H 26/27

Engine:	Modified camshaft, head gasket, Hartge valve cover, modified exhaust system, Hartge control unit.
Suspension:	Bilstein strut insert, sports spring front and rear, Bilstein rear shock absorber, strut brace. 35 mm lower.
Wheels/Tyres:	Alloy 7.5 x 16 195/50 VR 16 Pirelli P700 or 205/50 VR 16.
Brakes:	Modified brake pads, discs and calipers.
Miscellaneous:	Hartge footrest, gear knob, steering wheel, speedometer, monoarm windscreen wiper.
Performance:	148 mph

H5 3.4

Engine:	Modified camshaft, head gasket, Hartge valve cover, modified exhaust system, Hartge control unit.
Suspension:	Bilstein strut insert, sports spring front and rear, Bilstein rear shock absorber, strut brace. 35 mm lower.
Wheels/Tyres:	Alloy 7.5 x 16 215/55 VR 16 Pirelli P700 or 225/50 VR 16. Front – 8.5 x 17 235/45 ZR 17 Rear – 9.5 x 17 255/40 ZR 17.
Brakes:	Modified brake pads, discs and calipers.
Miscellaneous:	Hartge footrest, gear knob, steering wheel, speedometer, monoarm windscreen wiper.
Performance:	167 mph

H 6 SP

Engine:	Modified camshaft, pistons, Hartge valve cover, modified exhaust system with oval tailpiece, Hartge control unit.
Suspension:	Bilstein strut insert, sports spring front and rear, Bilstein rear shock absorber, strut brace, 35 mm lower.
Wheels/Tyres:	Front – Alloy 7.5 x 16 205/55 VR 16 Pirelli P700. Rear – Alloy 8.5 x 16 245/45 VR 16 Pirelli P700.
Miscellaneous:	Hartge footrest, gear knob, steering wheel, speedometer, monoarm windscreen wiper.
Performance:	165 mph

H7 3.4

Engine:	Modified camshaft, head gasket, Hartge valve cover, modified exhaust system, Hartge control unit.
Suspension:	Bilstein strut insert, sports spring front and rear, Bilstein rear shock absorber, strut brace. 20 mm lower.
Wheels/Tyres:	Alloy – 7.5 x 16 225/50 VR 16 Pirelli P700. Rear – 8.5 x 16 245/45 VR 16 Pirelli P700.
Miscellaneous:	Hartge footrest, gear knob, steering wheel, speedometer, monoarm windscreen wipe.
Performance:	162 mph

Griffin Motorsport

Was founded by Bill Griffin in 1986, a well known BMW racer who decisively won the '85 Modified Saloon Car Championship. All this practical competition experience has been incorporated in these British-based conversions.
Result: 220 bhp and 137 mph
320i/323i 2.3 litre engine conversion: modified cylinder head, performance camshaft, tubular exhaust manifold. Free flow exhaust system.
Result: 25 bhp increase on standard unit.

Griffin Sports suspension: Special lower springs, Bilstein gas filled dampers, anti-roll bars, strut braces.
Griffin Steering: High ratio steering rack (fewer turns lock to lock)

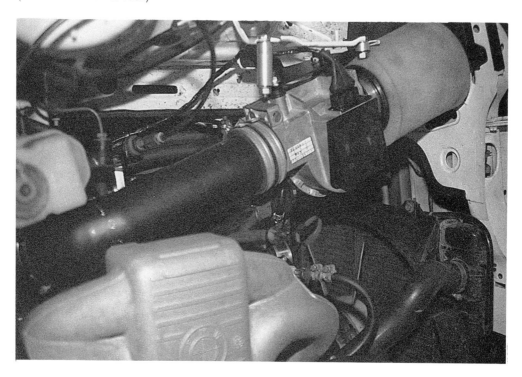

Supercharged

A performance option that you might not have considered is supercharging. A supercharger responds immediately, offering excellent boost at low speeds and the power available always matches the demands of the engine. A Scottish company, Fleming Thermodynamics have come up with the Sprintex screw compressor.

What is it?

The Sprintex consists of two rotors which are placed together in one casing, and mesh without touching. The casing has an inlet and outlet port positioned near the drive.

How does it work?

The larger of the rotors is driven by the engine via a toothed belt, subsequently driving the other through a set of helical gears.

What happens?

(a) The widest space between the rotors occurs at the inlet, which draws air in.
(b) This space is then closed by the end casing.
(c) As the rotors turn the air is forced along and compressed into the outlet port.

BMW Bodystyle

Your BM probably doesn't
look as sad as this example
which was found on the
streets of Munich, but help
is available to make your
car look a little different
and perhaps a little faster.

Spoilers, skirts, rear wing.
Hartge alloy wheels, splash
guards, underfloor
protection, badges and of
course the key fob that tells
everyone you're not driving
an 'ordinary' BMW.

Transform your old 02 into a Turbo
clone with wheel arch extensions, deep
front spoiler and Alpina alloy wheels.

BMW M Technic

BMW's own range of body kits and accessories for the whole range from 3 to 5 series designed by the motorsport department. So now you can turn your 316 into an M3 lookalike.

3 Series with spoilers, skirts, door mouldings, Zender Alloy wheels, with 'wing' aerodynamic moulding.

BUYING USED

The next best thing to a new BMW is probably a used one. They are built to last with both paintwork and upholstery, normally the first items to show signs of wear on other cars, holding up remarkably well for many years. BMW were one of the first manufacturers to realise that practicality and performance could prove to be a popular combination. Consequently prices on most models generally remain reassuringly high. Demand for good used BMs often outstrips supply, but it is still possible to buy these sporty saloons cost-effectively.

Maintaining a BMW can be expensive so unless you are an accomplished DIYer bear servicing costs in mind.

BMWs are safe cars and this means they have crumple zones. Repairs and insurance can be more than you budgeted for, so get quotes before you make a purchase.

On recent models, a full service history is essential to guarantee that the BMW has been properly maintained. Also a car with a service history will retain its resale value.

Whenever you look at a used BMW, try and take a friend with you to act as an objective eye and ear, i.e. to catch things you miss. Never rush a decision, always go away and think about it. Always drive the car and make sure that you look and listen to its performance and appearance. Don't be rushed. If you ever have doubts about any aspect of the car, don't buy it! Believe me there are plenty more BMWs that are just right for you.

It is possible to get the excellent manufacturer's used car warranty on BMWs that are up to five years old, with mileages of under 60,000 by taking them to an authorised agent and paying for a 25 point check. Cars that are within these parameters and bought from BMW dealers are automatically covered.

The following selection of BMW models serves as a general guide to their collectability and general durability with useful tips on what to look for.

Engine & transmission

Look where the car has been standing, or move it. Are there oil deposits?

Lift the bonnet and look inside. Examine the engine block as closely as you can; if not weather-protected they do crack. Check the radiator and oil level. If any of these fluids have mixed, the cylinder head gasket has probably blown. Start the engine from cold and listen for unwelcome noises from the timing chains, camshafts and tappets. Watch for excessive blue smoke from the exhaust, which can mean that the bores are worn. Once the engine is up to running temperature, with a cloth, remove the oil cap. Smokey fumes will mean that the engine needs a good overhaul.

Noisy exhaust? Replacing them is very expensive.

Engine

Being aluminium the unit is more sensitive to abuse, which usually means that the head gasket has failed. Check the fluid levels and the condition of the engine and assess for yourself whether the car has been looked after.

Power steering: with engine running turn wheel lock to lock, engine shouldn't stall. Also pump the brake, revs should drop slightly.

Automatic transmission with engine running apply brake and move gear selector through the D, N and R positions. There should be no audible 'clonks'. With brake still applied increase revs when in Drive or Reverse and car should rise at either end. On the road the transmission should respond smoothly. Have a look at the gearbox fluid; if dirty it indicates excessive wear.

On the drive: Listen for unusual rattles, creaks and knocks. Make sure that you investigate them thoroughly, although it can just be some loose items in the boot. Driving over rough ground will often reveal any suspension weaknesses, such as excessive pitching.

After the drive:

Tyres: Check for wear. If inside tread worn down this is an indication that the suspension is very worn.

Manual gearbox: The gear lever should move easily through the gears. There should be no excessive noise in first or reverse gears. Make sure that overdrive, when fitted, will engage. Car should pull away without too much complaint in second.

Inside: Make sure that you try out all the 'toys'. If the heater and air conditioning don't work, putting them right can be very expensive. Electric windows must travel smoothly to their fullest extents, as should sunroof. Carefully check the condition of the upholstery. Cracked, split or stained leather means an expensive re-trim. The same thing goes for damaged headlining and badly marked veneer on the dashboard.

Isetta 250/300/600

Production history

Debuted in 1955 with a 247 cc engine later increased to 297 cc. Some export models had just three wheels, but most had two wheels at the back placed close together.

At the end of 1957 a longer chassis with properly spaced wheels and a side door was introduced powered by a 582 cc twin cylinder developed from the R60 motorcycle unit.

Discontinued in 1962.

Mechanics

Ideally the oil should be changed every 1000 miles, so ask the owner. Don't force

gear lever into first, light pressure is all that is needed and it should operate smoothly. Look out for blue smoke which suggests wear and engine overhaul. Watch out for normal MOT failure points such as play in steering wheel, work bearings and drive couplings etc. n.b. Tyres and wheels from Mini can be utilised.

Bodywork

Rust attacks everywhere. Be careful when climbing in, the floor could be rotten! Otherwise check door and remaining bodywork.

Spares:

Limited supply, especially bodywork. You'll have to rely on remanufactures and used spares.

Comments & collectability:

Quite rare especially 600. Prices becoming high for restored models. To run them properly you really need the help of the Isetta Owners' Club.

700

Production history

Introduced in 1959 as 2 + 2 Coupé, followed by a cabriolet and two-door saloon with a 697 cc air-cooled twin-cylinder, producing 30 bhp. Sport option on the coupé and cabriolet had raised compression ratio and twin carburettors to produce 40 bhp.

For 1961 the longer wheelbased (6.3 inches) LX Luxus offered more room and was renamed BMW LS the next year and there was also a Coupé variant. 700 Sport becomes known as 700CS in '64.

Range discontinued in 1965.

Mechanics:

Gearbox always a bit notchy.

Bodywork:

Rust attacks the wheelarches, front panels and tail-light housings.

Spares:

Mechanics not so bad, but body panels a problem.

Comments & collectability:

Very rare car in UK. Prices not ridiculous because not appreciated in this country. Fast and reliable. Again the Isetta Owners Club will help.

1500/1600/1800/2000

Production history:

The 1500 four-door saloon with MacPherson strut front suspension with all new single overhead camshaft engine was introduced in 1962, followed by similar, but more powerful variants. It was succeeded by the 1600 in '64 with 3 bhp more.

For 1963 the new 1800 offered sporty TI (Touring International) with twin Solexes and increased compression ratio meant 100 bhp. 1600 TI also introduced. And in 1965 the TI/SA (which was originally available for competition use only) had twin Weber carburettors and produced 130 bhp.

The 2000 in 1966 distinguished by rectangular front headlamps and horizontal tail lights. Offered with 3-speed automatic. More powerful TI with twin Solex carburettors and increased compression ratio. TI Lux had luxurious interior which included walnut dashboard and plush upholstery.

Revised 1800 in 1968 has partly matt grille and buff chrome hubcaps. Later in 1971 1800 has fully blacked out grille, rectangular headlamps and tail lights, revised dashboard and improved dual circuit brakes.

2000tii in 1969 the first BMW with fuel injection had slotted hub caps.

Mechanics:

Transmission is a weak spot, so make sure that it moves easily through the gears. Listen for camshaft wear, rattling. Smoke usually indicates worn valve guides and oil seals. Fuel injection will give trouble if inexpertly tampered with.

Bodywork:

A lot of rot. Check everywhere. This includes wings, front panel, doors, sills, door shuts and hinge mounts. Lift carpet and look at floor pans, ditto boot.

Spares:

Mechanics are generally available although some body panels are becoming a problem.

Comments & collectability:

For the enthusiastic driver the TI, TI Lux and tii are the ones to go for, but the thing is that these are now very rare cars in the UK. Not noticeably appreciating in value, but stylish practical transport all the same.

1602/1502/1802/2002/ 02 Touring

Production history:

In 1966 a two-door version of the 4-door saloons but 500 pounds lighter, originally called the 1600-2. The following year more powerful 1600 TI was introduced along with an attractive Baur convertible.

2002 in 1968 had 2 litre single carburettor engine. In the same year a TI version offered 120 bhp. Automatic became an option in '69 with a three-speed ZF gearbox.

1971 saw many new models such as the 1802, 2002tii (with fuel injection) with cabriolet and touring (hatchback) versions.

Only 1600 2002 Turbos were made between 1973 and 1974, available in left-hand drive only in UK. Had larger fuel tanks, front spoiler and wheelarch extensions.

The 2002 and 1802 Tourings were discontinued in 1974 and in 1975 the rest of the range was deleted.

1502 from 1975 to '77 with 1573cc engine kept old style body alive.

Mechanics:

Smoky engine means worn valve guides and oil seals. Listen for rattling camshafts. Fuel injection plays up if not maintained properly. Transmission linkage mounting rubbers, rear tail shaft spline and rubber donut can give problems. The twin breaking often needs a full overhaul, discs, drums, hoses and back plates, particularly if the adjusters seize up.

Bodywork:

Rust is a problem so check front panel, door shut and hinge panels, wings outer and inner (open bonnet), sills (beware of over-sills that are merely cosmetic), floor pans, bonnet and boot. And on the Cabriolets check the drain holes (where hood frame sits) which often become blocked. Also if back of car sags the rear suspension springs and shock absorber mounts have probably corroded.

Spares:

Just about everything available with very few exceptions.

Comments & collectability:

Perhaps the best known and most popular of the older BMWs and prices certainly reflect this. In decending order of desirability 2002

65

Turbo rare and pricey, 2002tii Alpina version, 2002tii late (square tail lamps model), 2002 Cabriolets always popular, 2002ti, 2002 manual. Everything else not so popular, but shouldn't be discounted because this is very stylish and still fast, even the 1602, motoring.

2500/2800/3.0S/2.8L/3.0L/3.3L

Production history:

In 1968 the new six-cylinder saloons were introduced, with the twin carburettor 170 bhp 2500 and 192 bhp 2800. The 2800 was the more luxurious with limited slip differential and self-levelling rear suspension. Both were offered with automatic transmission as an option. These cars continued virtually unchanged until deletion in 1977.

The 3.0Si in 1972 had an increased 2985 cc displacement and D-Jetronic fuel injection.

Long wheelbase models (3″ extra) 2.8L, 3.0L and 3.3L introduced in 1974. All models were discontinued in 1977.

Mechanics:

Listen for signs of wear, particularly a rattling camshaft. Cars likely to have done a high mileage. Service history would be nice, but unlikely. A neglected fuel injection system where fitted could give problems.

Bodywork:

Check the wings, sills and floors for rust, especially door bottoms.

Spares:

Mechanical items are largely off the shelf. Many panels are interchangeable between models because they changed so little during production run.

Comments & collectability:

These cars do have a following, but not yet collectable in the ££££ sense. So it's possible to get a bargain. The bigger sixes offer considerable performance, so more fun than an early 7.

The Coupes 2000C – 3.0CSL

Production history

2 litre 2000C Coupé introduced 1965. The 2000CS had twin carburettors and higher rear axle ratio.

A longer chassis (75 mm) in 1968 housed the new six-cylinder engine and was called the 2800CS. Had more attractive and distinctive four headlamp frontal styling. It was replaced in 1971 by the 3.0CS larger engine, rear disc brakes and new Getrag four-speed gearbox. 3.0CSi had fuel injection and increased compression to produce 200 bhp.

3.0CSL (Coupé Sport Light) was a lightweight (aluminium doors, bonnet and bootlid) car intended for competition having distinctive spoilers and high rear wing.

In 1975 remaining CSL CSI and CS discontinued.

Mechanics:

On the four-cylinder 2000, knocking sounds mean a big end has gone. Listen for rattling camshafts on both four- and six-cylinder models. Suspect cylinder heads for cracking due to age. Engines need major overhaul once 80,000 miles clocked up. Worth checking that engine number matches chassis number to verify originality.

Bodywork:

Very prone to the red peril. Look for rust under front wings, floors, sills, around petrol tank and wheel arches.

Spares:

Mechanical parts are readily available, although some body panels are becoming scarce, particularly on the 2000. Alloy bonnet and boot lid no longer available for CSL.

Comments & collectability:

2000 has odd frontal styling that puts some people off, but few about. CS and CSi most popular and probably the most practical to own. 500 CSLs imported so very rare with 3.0CS with CSL spec. even more so, just 39 in total built.

3 Series

Production history – 1975–83

All new 3 series introduced in 1975. 316 had single headlamps. 320 had twin headlamps, 320i had K-Jetronic fuel injection, with automatic option.

In 1977 320 gets small M60 six-cylinder. Following year high performance 323i debuts.

For 1980 316 gets 1766 cc engine and Cabriolet made an option. 5-speed gearbox is standardised on 320 & 323i in 1982. Both models were discontinued that year. The 316 continued with a standard 5-speed until the middle of 1983.

1983–88

All new 3 Series introduced in 1983. Uninjected 1.8 litre called 316, injected version 318i, six-cylinder 320i and 323i. Four-door bodies appeared later that year. 323i has power increased from 139 bhp to 150 bhp.

In '84 4-speed automatic gearbox standard.

The 320i has output increased to 128 bhp in 1985. For 1986 the new Special Equipment model with headlamp wash/wipe, electric sunroof & windows, power steering, computer, alloy wheels and rear window blind are standard.

M3 introduced.

For 1987 revised front and rear treatment, 318i gets new M40 engine.

Mechanics:

Just listen for signs of wear particularly on old 3 Series. Notorious for camshaft wear. On all six cylinder cars watch for cracked cylinder head, oil in radiator coolant is giveaway. Clutch plates on later 3 series can go as early as 30,000 miles. Make sure that at least 4 green service interval indicator lights are on.

Bodywork:

New 3s shouldn't show any signs of rust. Older models suffer in usual places, sills, door bottoms, wings etc, but otherwise they wear very well. Be on guard for repairs after an accident – look at panel joins and for signs of overspray.

68

Spares:

No problem. Can be pricey though.

Comments & collectability:

No 3 series is presently collectable in the accepted sense. However the M3 and probably the early 323i are future classics. The six-cylinder cars can be expensive to run, particularly servicing. Don't dismiss the 316, it has the same superb build quality and cheaper maintenance.

5 Series

Production history – 1972–81

The new 5 series was launched with the 4-cylinder 2 litre engined 520 and 520i in

1972. The following year the 6-cylinder 2.5 525 was introduced, distinguished by bulge in bonnet and disc brakes all round. Power assisted steering was standard on the automatic. 518 arrives in 1975, but has smaller 1800 cc engine and was less well equipped. Automatic 518 only available from '77 to '78. High performance 528i has 2.8 litre engine, wood veneer door cappings and power-steering as standard.

For 1977 all models receive bonnet bulge, larger tail lights, forward mounted kidney grille and remote controlled door mirror.

In 1979 range gets electrically-operated driver's door mirror, digital clock and rear compartment heater.

1981–87 New body shape for all models; in 1981 service interval indicator. 528i Special Equipment has electric sunroof, computer and headlamp wash/wipe. Bosch K-Jetronic fuel injection with consumption meter.

525i gets L-Jetronic ignition in '83 and gets check control panel. Later that year the low revving fuel efficient 525 ETA introducted with Bosch Motronic engine management system and standard 4-speed automatic gearbox. Remainder of range get four-speed auto a year later.

518 becomes 518i in 1985 with L-Jetronic fuel injection, power steering and five-speed gearbox as standard.

New Lux models across range (except 528) with sunroof, green tinted glass, sports steering wheel, alloy wheels, rear head restraints and front fog lamps. Lux joined by

high performance 535i with 3.5 litre engine. M535i has M-Technic spoilers and suspension.

M5 in 1986 has Motorsport engine with manual close ratio gearbox as standard. In same year 535i replaced by 535iSE.

Models discontinued in 1988.

Mechanics:

Check for wear, particularly camshaft, and cracked cylinder heads. Power-steering is expensive to replace, so carry out relevant test.

Bodywork:

The old 5 if neglected rusts in all the usual places – wings, doors and sills etc. Newer 5s, just watch for stone chips.

Spares:

No problems.

Comments & collectability:

518 is the least popular, although the 518i was a big improvement. 525e most

underrated, yet offers performance with startling economy. 520is most common. 535i from 1980 becoming collectable and later version along with M5 will probably follow, but still expensive. Servicing not cheap.

6 Series

Production history

New coupés for 1976 were the 630 CS and 633 CSi (only in UK). The 633 had a 3210 cc unit producing 200 bhp. This power output was increased with the introduction of the 635 CSi in 1978 to 218 bhp. Distinguished by larger front and rear spoilers.

633 discontinued in 1979 and 628 CSi smaller engined coupé for 1980 with power steering, electric windows and central locking as standard. In the same year 635 gets the electronic engine management system.

Styling changes for 1982 include revised bumpers, side mouldings and spoiler. Engine receives L-Jetronic injection. 635 gets rear spoiler, four-speed automatic, ABS braking, metallic paint and computer as standard. 628 gets ABS in 1984 and discontinued in 1987.

M635 with Motorsport engine and M-Technic body kit introduced in 1985.

1987 models get the new 7s engine, tyres and switchable gearbox.

Mechanics:

6-cylinder weak spots of camshaft and splitting block. Older cars without service history should be treated with caution.

Bodywork:

They must rust eventually, but mostly looked after well, apart from chips and scratches.

Spares:

No problems.

Comments & collectability:

Expensive to run. Beware cheap early cars, they need lots spent to make them reliable. 628 never really popular. M635 classic for the future. However 633 looks the same, take off the badge and put on non-year registration plate and spoilers and who's to know that you haven't spent £30,000 + ?

7 Series

Production history

All new big saloons introduced in 1977. 728, 730 and fuel injected 733i make up the range.

In 1979 728 gets fuel injection, the 730 is replaced by the 732i and 733i by the 735i. For 1980 service interval indicator standard on range both 732i and 735i get electronic management systems. 735i Special equipment has metallic paint, air-conditioning, computer, cruise control etc as standard.

ABS braking becomes standard in 1982 on the 735i, optional on other models. September '82 re-style of grille and spoiler.

Special equipment versions (similar to 735) of 728i and 732i.

Models discontinued in 1986.

Mechanics:

Listen for wear, smoky exhaust and rattling camshaft. Power-assisted steering must function effectively. Make sure that all the toys work, air-conditioning, electric windows, etc.

Bodywork:

No real rust problems, but on older models check wings, sills and wheel arches.

Spares:

No problems.

Comments & collectability:

Service history should be reassuring. 732is never popular, so could be a bargain. Level of specification on the Special Equipment models very high. None particularly collectable – yet.

BMW TODAY

BMW entered the 1980s with a very successful and attractive range of cars. From the popular 3 series, through to the luxurious 7 and exclusive M1, BMW had a line-up they could be proud of. However, BMW did not rest on their laurels and have continued to develop the range.

5 series 81–87

In 1981 the 5 series, which had changed little from its introduction, was the first model to be fully revamped. BMW had started work on a second generation design in 1975, code named E–28.

Bodywork

Only the central body structure was carried over from the old car, although the shape remained familiar. But it was more aerodynamic and much lighter.

Engines

The power plants were also reworked to increase power and economy, with six-cylinder models getting L-Jetronic fuel injection.

Technology

The 5s also pioneered the revolutionary service interval indicator, a computerised system that tells you when the car needs a service.

5 Series 1988

BMW totally redesigned their mid-range saloon which with minor developments will probably last into the next century.

Bodywork

2 inches wider and 4 inches longer than the earlier car. The drag coefficient of the all new body varies between 0.30 and 0.32, depending on the model.

Engines

These have the latest Digital Motor Electronics (DME) with a new 2986 cc unit for the 530 and the 535 sharing the 735's engine.

Technology

The latest three channel Bosch ABS braking. Automatic Stability Control (ASC) and Engine Override Control (EOC) monitors the friction between tyre and the road, so that the right amount of power is used with no loss of handling.

3 Series 1983

More crucial for BMW was the continued success of its 3 series range. Again they followed the same policy of developing a proven design and incorporating advanced technological features.

Bodywork

Completely redesigned and more aerodynamic.

Engine

All models from the 318i up, got L-Jetronic ignition and with the high performance 323i acquired the Bosch Motronic engine management system constant state of tune. The 318i got an all new engine in 1987 and shares the same cylinder head design as the 750i!! 115 bhp and 115 mph.

Range

3 Series was also developed into a more practical car with the introduction of four-door models. The high performance M3, 325iX four-wheel drive and Touring broadened the appeal.

Future

New 3 series similar in appearance to 3 and 5 series expected in the early '90s.

7 Series 1983–87

An uprated version of the 7 series was introduced in September 1983. Fuel consumption was reduced across the range by revising the front end which improved the drag factor. Mechanical changes included the adoption of a four-speed automatic gearbox.

1987

After 7 years' development the new 7 has set new standards in the luxury car market. An even sleeker body means a very low 0.32 drag. A fully revised six-cylinder engine with the latest electronic management system has led to power with economy.

Future

Like the 5 series, seems set to take BMW confidently into the next century.

6 Series

M635 retained its classic shape, but under the skin sports suspension, ABS, on-board computer and four-speed automatic were included in the package from 1983. The very high performance M package arrived in '85 with the 24 valve M1 engine. In 1987 it got the 735i's power unit.

Future

About to be replaced by a new generation of BMW Coupés. What a difficult act to follow!

Car

Z1

Bodywork

Glass fibre with doors that slide into the high side sill by an electro-mechanical system. Drag coefficient 0.34 with hood up, 0.42 with hood down. An undertray provides optimum airflow beneath the car to give true 'ground effect' properties, so it sticks to the road!

Technical

Powered by the 325i's engine which is positioned behind the front wheels to achieve almost perfect weight distribution 49/51%. An all-new Z arm rear suspension set-up makes for even better road holding.

Heritage

Carries on the tradition of the 328 and 507.

Future

Not destined to be built in right-hand drive, or be sold in the UK – at the moment.

Eberhard Von Kuenheim

Significance

The longest serving Chairman in the motor industry, who has built BMW into one of the most respected and stable companies in the world.

Early years

A mechanical engineering degree in the 1950s resulted in a number of managerial positions within that industry. In 1965 Herbert Quandt took him on as a technical advisor for the Quandt manufacturing empire.

In charge

January 1st 1970 was the day when Kuenheim became the Chairman of BMW. If his progress to the top was remarkable, then so was his age, just 42. Although the company was successful when he took his place on the board, there is no doubt that BMW's commitment to growth and technological advances can be attributed to his leadership.

Future

Kuenheim is firmly in control at BMW and there is no reason why he can't confidently steer the company long into the '90s.

The V12 story

It's a brave motor manufacturer that designs and builds an engine with twelve cylinders. But the concept of a Grosser (Big) BMW is one that has preoccupied them for many years.

V12 I

1965: The brief was to build a V8 and the answer was simply to join two of the existing four-cylinder units. When fitted to a coupé the performance was incredible, reaching speeds in excess of 155 mph.

1972: Project abandoned because of tooling costs. Also a new engine development programme had begun.

V12 II

1972: Again it involved joining existing units together. This time it was the M-60 small block six that was destined for the 3 and 5 series. A V12 appealed to the BMW board for many reasons, but the best reason was that Mercedes Benz didn't have one.

1974: The M66 programme was dropped once the implications of the fuel crisis became apparent.

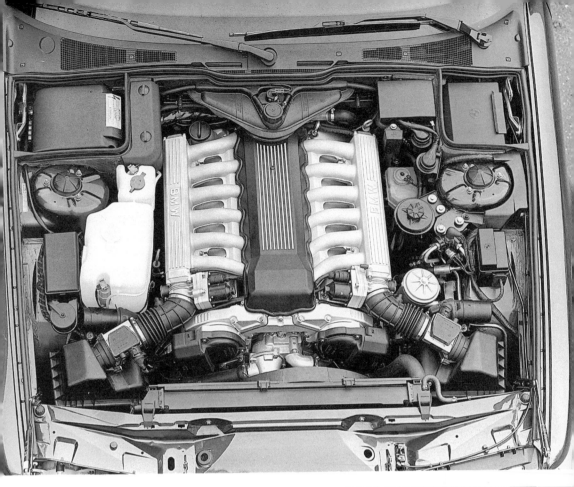

V12 III

1982: December, BMW started from scratch to produce an all-new V12. More than 2500 individual parts needed to be designed.

1983: The engine runs for the first time.

1983–85: 400 prototype engines later, the V12 was ready to be run in the new 7 series.

1986–87: Extensive road testing. The fruits of this development was a 4988 cc V12 producing 300 bhp at 5200 rpm, with 3rd generation Motronics to keep the engine operating automatically at its optimum output.

The future

This remarkable engine has now been mated with some remarkable cars. The 750i and 850i. Mercedes are about to introduce a V12 unit of their own. Need any more be said?

In the UK

With an on-the-road price that comfortably exceeds £50,000 the 200 unit allocation was sold even before the price was announced.

Building a BMW, steps 1–8

Building a BMW takes time. What starts as a tightly wound coil of steel takes three shifts or one and a half days to transform into a highly finished product that we all recognise as a quality car.

1. That coil of steel is taken to the press shop. Once there blanks are cut from the sheet metal and shaped by the deep draw presses into the major body components of the car.

2. From there the floor panels, side frames, door panels and roofs are bolted, brazed and joined together by the automated multi-welders.

3. The next stage is the paint shop. If you wondered why the BMW's bodywork is so good, the secret is in the preparation.
(a) The body is degreased and cleaned.
(b) The bare metal is coated with zinc phosphate. (c) With an electrode attached, submerged into a bath of water-soluble paint.
(d) Primer is applied by cataphoresis which is then baked on. (e) Robots then spray on a PVC underseal. (f) The next coat of paint follows with filler applied electrostatically.
(g) Each body will then enter drying tunnels, where temperatures exceed 100°C, after every coat of paint, baking the colour onto the metal. (h) When the machines have finished, it is skilled craftsmen who return to "buff down" the bodywork. (i) Again the bodies are sprayed by machine to add more coats of paint. (j) The final stage consists of the application of a special wax that will provide long-lasting protection against corrosion.

4. As for the engines, BMW cast the cylinder heads and most of the other aluminium parts at their own foundry. Engine blocks, crankshafts and other steel parts are delivered by suppliers as blanks. These are then

machined, assembled, tuned and checked. The engine is then bolted to the gearbox.

5. The suspension components are also produced by BMW. So spring struts, brakes, differentials and shafts are then mounted on axle carriers to make the finished assembly.

6. On the inside seats and interior panels are fashioned in BMW's own upholstery shops.

7. Finally all of these parts come together, often from different plants and suppliers. The painted bodies acquire windows, instruments, seats, headlights, bumpers and the famous kidney grille. The installation of engine and axle units into the body takes just 30 seconds.

8. The only other essentials to help the new BMW roll off the production line are the wheels, oil and fuel. Then the pre-delivery checks can begin.

BMW ADVERTISING

Amongst the hundreds of car ads produced every year there are just a few manufacturers who manage to make their advertisements stand out. BMW is one of the very best, developing memorable, stylish and often amusing campaigns. The thought behind this series of promotional photographs for the BMW Isetta seems to be that the little car will look after you from the cradle to the grave. Well, at least the intervening years between those events.

If you're fed up with trying to find a space near the exit in Tesco's car park, then the BMW Isetta is the answer. No bigger than the average superstore trolley, you can now pick up your groceries without leaving the driving seat. Is this the ultimate shopping machine?

Yes that's right, no need to worry about being late for that vital dinner engagement. With the BMW Isetta you can pull right into the restaurant and made it a cosy evening for three.

What every newly wed couple craves for, a warm, dry confined space, with shock absorbers ready to take the strain. Now they can get on with the honeymoon. But how long will it last?

83

However, in more recent years BMW have set the advertising standard for the motor industry. Their agency WCRS Mathews Marcantonio annually visit the factory in Munich and in Account Manager Steve Bliss's words, "look out for little nuggets of information, or stories which best exemplify BMW values and standards." Here's what they mean.

The bodywork

The first thing you notice on a BMW is the superb paintwork. In fact, the first thing you notice on an old BMW is the paintwork. Not surprisingly a quarter of the time spent building a BMW is taken up by a thorough 46 stage paint process (see *Building a BMW*). The first stage of any anti-corrosion process is to ensure that the original sheet metal is of the highest quality, hence 'IT SEEMS A SHAME TO PAINT IT'.

There's a PVC undercoat which ensures that if stones or other objects do chip away the surface paintwork, the bare metal is never exposed. So one can well believe that they've 'ADDED A COAT OF ELASTIC'. On the same subject, PVC. The shotgun really was used to test the effects of stone chips. When BMW say they spray it, they SPRAY IT.

YOU'LL BE SURPRISED WHAT WILL BOUNCE OFF A BMW
NOW WE'VE ADDED A COAT OF ELASTIC.

TO PROVE A BMW IS RUSTPROOF
SPRAY IT.

Awards

All these paintwork ads won gold awards for the best colour campaign in the 1986 Advertising Awards.

The engine

Start a BMW and you'll have trouble hearing it tick-over. The build quality is second to none. The surface of the cylinders is actually

85

cross-hatched using diamonds, whilst many manufacturers rely on less accurate ceramic cutting tools. So a BMW must be FOREVER. The theme of the previous ad is continued as even more precious objects are revealed to be part of the process of making a precious piece of machinery. Rubies are used in the laser measuring equipment. Platinum is used in the air metering device. Gold and silver are used for the electrical contacts. Obviously the engine is a GEM.

**WHY DO WE USE THEM ON OUR CYLINDERS?
(BECAUSE A BMW IS FOREVER.)**

THE ULTIMATE DRIVING MACHINE

**"WHAT CAR?" CALLED THE ENGINE A GEM.
THEY OBVIOUSLY KNOW WHAT GOES INTO IT.**

THE ULTIMATE DRIVING MACHINE

More awards

Again this was the best colour campaign (shame this book's in black and white).

South of France not only revealed that the weather and lifestyle is very agreeable in that part of the world, but also that the quantity of BMWs on the Côte d'Azur sea front could

SPORTS CAR OR ESTATE CAR.
HAVE BMW STRUCK
THE PERFECT BALANCE?

THE ULTIMATE DRIVING MACHINE

The range

For the launch of the Touring the advertising objective was to make sure that it didn't come across as another boring estate car (a BMW?!?!) In effect it's a sports car (135 mph) with handling to match (50/50 weight distribution) and a bigger boot. Certainly not an estate car, a word that is almost totally banned by BMW. The perfect balance, achieved.

An ad agency fact-finding mission to the

lead to only one conclusion. BMW owners would rather drive their 528s to the Med than fly, sail or anything else.

And whilst in the Côte the ad agency team probably encountered the 40 lucky owners of the exclusive M635. That's right, just 40 are allocated to be sold each year in the UK. Some of us are dreaming, others are busy saving.

87

WHY DO SO MANY BMWS FLY SOUTH IN THE SUMMER?

THE ULTIMATE DRIVING MACHINE

ANYONE CAN DREAM, ONLY 40 CAN BUY.

THE ULTIMATE DRIVING MACHINE

April fool

A word of warning, don't take the following ads too seriously. Each April 1st for the last few years a light-hearted jape from BMW brightens the pages of the national press. Often it is much more successful than the newspaper's official red herrings.

Conception

A competition is held whereby the objective of that ad is distributed throughout the agency and the winner is chosen by the creative director.

600 people responded to this ad replying to Uve Vörlen Vörrit (geddit?!?!). They received a genuine BMW conversion kit which included sticky BMW logos with the roundel reversed to stick on the wheel hubs, boot, bonnet and steering wheel.

This time Uve Beenhad was prepared to provide you with more details of the unique badge cleaning system. Another astounding success which proves that motor manufacturers do have a sense of humour.

NOW THE BMW MARQUE WILL NEVER BE MARKED.

It has been said that when a person invests in a BMW, they're really paying for a name.

It's a charge that BMW have long learned to live with.

After all, BMW is a name that reflects the very highest standards of construction and the very pinnacle of technical excellence.

Sadly, layers of grime and dirt combine to leave it a name reflecting little else.

Nowhere more so than on the enamel bonnet badge.

So in a bid to keep their nose clean, BMW have developed the Badgewash system.

Available as standard on the new 750iL (and as an option on all other models) it features technology never seen on a car before.

A tiny sensor mounted in the wiper arm measures the light reflected back from the white sections of the BMW badge.

Even if a film of dirt cuts out as little as 5% of that light, the sensor will detect it and start the wiper.

The system is closely linked to the acclaimed Motronic engine management system. It means the wipe pressure can actually change depending on the car's speed.

The jet washer boasts equally futuristic technology.

An ion exchange system softens the water before it's sprayed onto the badge.

(Hard water would of course scratch the enamel surface.)

A fine system, you'll agree. But it's only the tip of the iceberg. BMW are refining a boot Badgewash at their German Research and Development complex.

Plans are in the pipeline for a wheel Badgewash utilising pressure from the brake pipe.

There's even talk of an anti-static steering wheel badge for dustier climes.

Clearly, BMW will go to extraordinary lengths to clear their name.

Send to Uve Beenhad, BMW Information Service, PO Box 46, Hounslow, Middlesex TW4 6NF. Please send me more details of the BMW.
☐ Badgewash ☐ Bootwash ☐ Wheelwash ☐ Hajiwash

Name

Address

Postcode

THE ULTIMATE DRIVING MACHINE

This time Uve Adjurl-Egpüld had the last laugh with this very logical solution to the problems of continental touring. The author remembers this one with particular affection because he sold BMWs at the time and had carefully to assist those who took it too seriously, to see the funny side.

WHEN YOU CROSS THE CHANNEL, OUR STEERING WHEEL CROSSES OVER WITH YOU.

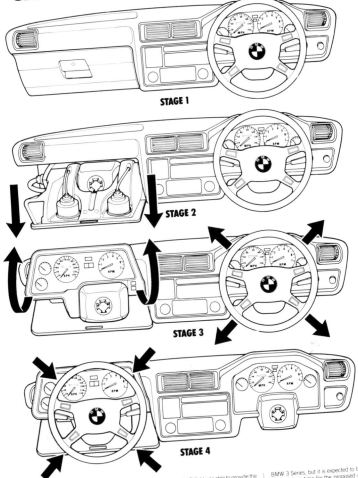

STAGE 1

STAGE 2

STAGE 3

STAGE 4

Since the 'Droit de Seigneur' act, passed in 1867, the French have always driven on the right-hand side of the road.

This is not merely a matter of inconvenience for British drivers, it is also a potential safety hazard. And yet car manufacturers have been ignoring the problem completely.

With one notable exception. Because BMW engineer Aap Rilfuhl discovered, just three years ago, that the problem could be tackled, and, with ingenious modifications, a test vehicle was designed that incorporated a unique BMW feature – the multi-dashboard facility.

By incorporating a second-unit steering wheel socket and instrument panel into a conventional glove compartment, Dr Rilfuhl was able to provide the basis for a secondary driving position.

The fascia, naturally enough, conforms to 'Continental' standards – with a kph speedometer, and the 'Lawson' fuel gauge reading in litres.

Then, by the insertion of a lynch-pin into the steering wheel column, fellow engineer Hans Grabbem was able to devise the first quick-release steering wheel (incorporated, too, into the column is a secondary 'Continental' horn – the 'Vonn-Drivers' 80 decibel air-horn.)

The final problem, of the foot-pedals, was easily resolved, Herr Grabbem made them transferable, too, with a dual position facility.

At present, this option is only available on the BMW 3 Series, but it is expected to be available on all models in time for the proposed opening of the Channel tunnel.

And then, for the first time, British drivers will be able to drive abroad without getting on the wrong side of the natives.

THE ULTIMATE DRIVING MACHINE

BMW Motorcycles

But for motorcycles, BMW wouldn't be building cars today. The foundation of their success was a range of motorcycles that were not only exciting, but way in advance of any other machine. After all, the life-saving, or BMW-saving, Isetta and 700 series were motorcycle based.

The K Series story

BMW is now one of only a handful of companies who build both quality cars and motorcycles. And it was to car technology that BMW turned in order to produce their most advanced range of bikes.

Why?

Aware that many manufacturers had caught up, and were beginning to make the BMWs seem like 'old men's' bikes, they started the design with a clean sheet.

Car power

As a fundamental departure from the flat-twin layout they opted for a car engine. For experimental and trial purposes BMW chose the 945 cc unit that powered the Peugeot 104.

Layout

It was laid flat with the crankshaft on the right side of the frame. This layout meant that the rotation took place on the same plane, from crankshaft, to gearbox, to propshaft. The traditional drive shaft was retained, BMW wouldn't permit anything as crude as a chain! This concept was so original that BMW immediately filed a patent for it and the BMW Compact Drive System was born. The production K100 unit was to be made by BMW as either an in-line 3- or 4-cylinder water-cooled engine, another departure.

Advanced

Like their cars BMW also made great use of advanced electronics which included a breakerless distributor and Bosch LE-Jetronic control.

Successful

When production commenced in October 1983 the K100 was quite clearly the ultimate riding machine.

Powerful

The lightness of the engine and its low position in the frame contribute to the excellent performance of the machine. Although BMW are cagey about true top speeds, it will certainly exceed 130 mph and power up to 60 mph in about 4 seconds!

Safe

But not only is the BMW one of the world's fastest motorcycles, it's also one of the safest, thanks to the revolutionary ABS braking system. Irrespective of how hard you brake, the system regulates the front and rear brakes independently of one another. As a result the bike slows without the wheels locking.

Sum up

The K series bikes may cost as much as an ordinary car, but for that money you'll get an extraordinary motorcycle.

The rest of the range

R100 RS/RT R80 RT R80 R65, K series technology with the Boxer engine.

R100 GS R80 GS Trial bikes.

Historically

When the motorcycle's centenary was celebrated in 1985 not surprisingly it was the BMWs that represented the most significant technical advances, and their riders had snazzier leather gear!

For all ages and in all ages

Ernst Henne the most famous BMW racer of the '30s and '50s sampling today's K100 whilst probably remembering earlier years when things weren't so comfortable.

Here's a selection of often rather tall tales that might make you smile, chuckle, gasp, or just shake your head in disbelief. But what they all have in common of course is one thing. That's right, a BMW.

There are several golden rules that you've got to observe when piloting a BMW Bubble Car.

Never put anything in the boot – there isn't one.

Avoid leaning in any direction when cornering – the Bubble is likely to trip up and fall over.

Restrict the number of passengers to one – otherwise it is likely to steam up in winter and you won't be able to see where you're going.

Steer around tram lines, deep gutters and prominent man hole covers – it's easy for Bubbles to get stuck in a rut.

And perhaps the most important rule . . . well, let's see what happened to Richard Burgess when he borrowed his brother's Bubble.

When Richard had made the date to take Linda to see *Close Encounters of the Third Kind* he knew that travelling by bus wouldn't exactly create the right impression. His brother's old Isetta 250 cc probably wouldn't either, but at least it would get them there, back and somewhere quiet in between, if everything went well.

Everything did go well, from picking up Linda, who was delighted to be offered a door-to-door service, right up until they got into the car park. He'd forgotten the most golden of golden BMW Bubble rules:

Never park facing an inanimate object – you could be stuck there for quite some time.

In that quietest and darkest part of the cinema car park, Richard quickly discovered that the single door only opened outwards, but only as far as the facing brick wall would allow – 3 inches. The fact that the BMW was not fitted with a reverse gear didn't help. The people at whom Richard and Linda shouted and waved as they filed out of the cinema merely did the same back.

They were rescued in the early hours of the following morning by a friendly milkman called Roger. However, the enforced confinement and close encounter with a brick wall didn't bring them together mentally or physically. No happy ending, wedding, or embarrassing event 9 months later . . .

A BMW is a pretty rare sight anywhere in Russia and near Smolensk, almost unheard of, yet Sergei Tambov was lucky enough to find one in 1985. Admittedly it wasn't complete, having been abandoned by an Italian tourist once an electric fault had reduced it to a charred shell.

The car in question was a 1973 1802 Touring now finished in a rather charred henna red. The 1600 engine had already been taken and was probably installed in a tractor by the time he came across the BM. To convert it for his own use, Sergei stripped the shell of all the unnecessary interior and mechanical parts. Everything was hand painted red, and the interior trimmed in carpet. Apart from the shell, all that was left were the wheels.

To complete the job, all Sergei had to do was get his horse used to pulling a rather unusual cart! Having spent several fruitless years on the waiting list for a new Moskvich, a one horse power BMW seemed like a better alternative. Perfect for local journeys.

And as for the kidney grille, where else could it go except around the horse's neck!

The BMW with the absolute mostest can currently be found in the Gulf State of Kuwait. It was ordered by an unidentified but obviously very well off gentleman who resides there. The modifications were carried out by a number of specialist coachbuilders in Britain, Germany and France in the utmost secrecy. Not surprisingly it became known as the "Beast".

A 745i, the turbo 7 series was used as the base car and the specification included 2" armour plating surrounding the rear passenger areas; special metallic strawberry red paintwork; gold plated chrome; 3 halogen

headlamps; Hartge bodykit; Hartge alloy wheels; 2 x 3.5 turbo engines; 8 wheel drive; buffalo leather upholstery; gold plated accessories; directional radar (in case you get lost!); television, video, satellite dish; 300 watt sound system; 2 x BMW R100 GS motorcycles.

Yes really, two motorcycles are packed flat and occupy the boot space. When required they can be removed and mounted in just 30 seconds!

The rumour is that work has almost finished on a new 7 finished to an even more outlandish specification. Expect to see that featured in *BMW Driver's Book II!*

This is George Halliday's faithful BMW Isetta. It cost him just 300 DMs in 1974 and provided a practical and economic means of commuting around Munich. It also proved to be extremely cost-effective right from day one because he sold the spares that came with the car for 200 DMs!

It has since taken him all over Europe on many long-distance trips without a hint of trouble. He always carries plenty of spares and on the day he took me for a ride through Munich, there was a spare exhaust system rattling around on the rear shelf. You have to be careful when getting in, because you could find yourself standing in the road surrounded by a rusty floor pan. Otherwise the engine pulls you along enthusiastically.

Mr. Halliday, an expatriate Scot, is actually used to much more exotic machinery, especially as he has worked for the last fifteen years at BMW. But as attractive as a company 7 series might be, it won't squeeze into postage stamp parking spaces, or do 60 miles to the gallon.

Driving a Bubble car is an experience in itself and Mr. Halliday compared it to his RAF days when he flew Meteor jet aircraft! I think it is the cockpit-like interior, rather than the performance, that led to this unique conclusion.

When the Philippines dictator, President Marcos was relieved of his duties much publicity was made of the finds in the Presidential Palace.

However, two rather interesting items were apparently overlooked, because amongst the piles of footwear were two BMW 316s belonging to Imelda Marcos. You could tell they were Imelda's because they were finished in metallic pink, her favourite, colour and every badge bore the legend IMELDA, if you were still in any doubt.

Inside, the roof lining was trimmed in mink with gold-plated trim and mother-of-pearl inlaid dashboard. The mileometer readings

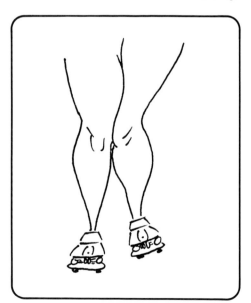

registered just 1548 on one and 892 on the other, so they never went very far.

But why did she need two BMWs finished in exactly the same way? Well, as one Filipino wag commented at the time they were found, she had one for each foot.

The whereabouts of these very special BMWs are presently unknown.

Getting a dent in your kidney grille is a very painful experience. It's also very expensive and very annoying. Bill Murray's BMW had suffered from the parking-by-feel antics of others and had the scars to prove it. That's why he decided to set up an import company to acquire these vital items. However, he didn't go to the official source, Munich. He went instead to a very unofficial one, Taiwan.

A contact had assured him that a small manufacturing company there that specialised in vacuum forming would be able to help, and sure enough when Murray telephoned they were most helpful. It was agreed that the kidney grilles be made in plastic. They would still look authentic yet be cheap. The purist could use it as an interim replacement, whilst skinflints could save a few bob.

The minimum production run was 50,000 units and Murray readily agreed. Already he had several American and European wholesalers who were willing to take bulk orders and in the UK he planned to start a mail order operation.

With these guarantees of success in mind, Murray upped the order to 100,000 then sat back and wondered how to spend the profits.

On opening the first crates in his Midlands warehouse Murray's first reaction was to check his calendar to see that it wasn't April 1st. Inside were a large number of bowls. Painted correctly – black with silver edges. Apparently something had been lost in the translation. Murray had 100,000 two-tone kidney bowls on his hands.

Australian Kenny Masters is both an enthusiastic wine and BMW lover, but not necessarily in that order. He lives in the Hunter Valley, New South Wales, one of the richest wine producing areas in that country. This perfect location allows him to cultivate a few vines and bottle a very cheeky red in the process.

His present pride and joy is an Australian specification 528i finished in metallic red. The name of that colour is Burgundy. Consequently Kenny takes a few liberties and calls his 'brew' burgandy (Australian spelling to reflect the Australian pronunciation).

For the buffs it is made from Shiraz grapes, which Kenny really knows how to look after when they're on the vine. Being produced in small quantities the results are excellent. Rich, some might say sweaty in aroma, the wine mellows with age. It takes about 5 years to reach full maturity. "Gentle yet rich" is how one lucky Australian taster has described it. So to mindlessly sup Kelly's BM Burgandy at a casual barby (Australian for barbecue) would be quite wrong. But that's exactly what Kenny does every weekend.

With annual production running at little more than five cases a year it's unlikely ever to reach our shores.

DAS BMW BOOT!

als Sicherheitszelle konzipiert
mit auf Stoßstangenhöhe plat-
zierten Flankenschutz-
in den Türen. Die Se

gen Ablagemöglichkeiten für
Kleinutensilien in den Seiten-
ableckungen und in ver-
schließbaren Fächern
sind

funktionen der Scheibenwi-
scher (automatisches Dauer-
wischen, der Heckscheibe
beim Einlegen des Rück-
wärt werden

Here's an article that was recently published in the German press. Roughly translated, it claims that an engineering professor from Augsburg has built a water-going M1!

Apparently the fibreglass construction of the bodywork makes it the perfect base for conversion to an M1 speedboat. The requisite BMW marine technology means that much of the existing propeller and ancillary equipment is available. Obviously the exhaust has to be re-routed to finish above the water line. However, ballast tanks and improved sealing is required to keep everything afloat and dry inside.

So far only preliminary testing has taken place and although the detailed results are being kept secret, observers report that speeds in excess of 30 knots have been achieved. The present development programme will ensure that that speed will increase quite significantly.

So what's the purpose of all this? Well, European motor industry researchers have identified a very strong demand for amphibious cars. The final cost is likely to be very high, but people are eager to buy. Already Professor Ripple has received many offers for his prototype. Driving down to the sunny Med. is one thing, but being able to drive straight in is quite another. Such a car, whether or not it came in the shape of an M1, really would be the ultimate status symbol.

As to who will eventually construct these amphibious supercars, the indications are that a small specialist builder would be the obvious choice. And as Britain has one of the largest glass fibre body building industries in the world, there's no reason why it couldn't all be started over here.

Who needs the stuffy Channel Tunnel when an M1 would whisk you straight across to France in half the time and twice the style?

German rock band 'Von Shocker' have a close affinity with BMWs. As lead singer Rudi Heitz told me, "The Mercedes is either an old man's car or a truck. A Porsche is for men with chest hair, you know what I'm saying. An Audi is for people who can't afford anything better. VWs, I mean, what's the point? But the BMV is a way of life."

Just how closely associated Von Shocker have become with BMWs is displayed in many of their songs. Here's an extract from one of their ditties entitled "Where's the petrol":

Cruising down the autobahn/With Heidi at my side
Just two hundred kilometres/let's see if she'll slide
In my BMV/A supercharged three/Supercharged three.
In my BMV/You'll never catch me/You'll never catch me.
©Von Shocker Sounds 1987.

Although their following is very selective, it is growing all the time. Some of their more enthusiastic fans buy 2002s, 3.0 saloons, or coupés, paint them black, put the band's logo on the bonnet and install a Blaupunkt New

von shocker!

York sound system and then of course play Von Shocker's tapes. When the fans get together they drive in convoy through the cities where the band is playing.

The Band's cars: Rudi Heitz (lead singer) 3.0CSL. Manfred Manther (drums) 2002tii. Peter Verner (guitar) 2002 Turbo. Klaus Harmer (guitar/keyboards) 2800CS. All are finished in black.

n.b The M******S articulated truck that carries their equipment has had its three-pointed star substituted by a kidney grille.

Alan Bennet is a motor fanatic. In fact, he originally trained as a mechanic. However, his colleagues soon discovered that the delicious results he achieved with sausages, beans, eggs and a loaf of bread, were better than his efforts with a socket set. Consequently he moved into the fast food business.

But Alan found it difficult not to involve motor cars in some way. Indeed, to put excitement into sandwich and snack making, each creation had often unique ingredients and an appropriate motoring name.

One of Alan's favourite makes of cars was the BMW which he always made a special effort to service properly.

BMW Burgers, 750 fritters and M Power Pies have interesting and often very genuine Bavarian ingredients such as sauerkraut and schnitzel to make them go with a bang.

the first thing he did was slam the BMW into the car parked in front.

What Roger hadn't realised was that a totally white dashboard would reflect directly onto the windscreen. Not surprisingly the forward view would resemble a particularly bad blizzard. Rather than remove the winds-creen, or drive with his head poking out of the sunroof, Hallam decided to have the top of the dashboard painted black.

To this day Mrs Hallam refuses to travel in a car she's nicknamed 'The Iceberg'. Can we blame her? . . .

Lord Wraxhall was the unfortunate victim of burglary at his home. But having disturbed the raiders he was kidnapped, locked in the boot of his 5 series and dumped several miles away.

Roger Hallam wanted a white car. Not only that, he wanted a white BMW, and the white cars he'd seem just weren't white enough. To his eyes the success of such a colour, or non-colour, scheme meant that a total white-out was necessary to create the desired effect. So when he ordered his new 635 there were no half measures. Alpine White paint-work, chrome, door mirrors, windscreen wipers, bumpers and wheels. On the inside white leather, carpets and dashboard completed the all-white picture.

When delivery day came Roger Hallam was more than pleased with the result; even so,

He managed to smash out the light clusters to make sure of fresh air supply. There he remained for seven very uncomfortable and probably quite terrifying hours. When finally released by the police the only comment Lord Wraxhall had on his ordeal was – "Good grief, there's more room in the back than I ever thought."

Not everyone likes the look of a BMW. Surprised? Well apparently the old 4-door 1500 – 2000 series bears an uncanny resemblance to the Iron Curtain Ladas! That's why they are unpopular restoration projects!!!

There was almost a British BMW Museum.

The UK concessionaires in the late '70s were ambitious enough to consider setting up a showcase for BMWs that would be second only to Munich's splendid collection. However, with just a few cars acquired like the superb 503 below, with matching number plates, the idea was abandonded. (photo courtesy Sotheby's)

CELEBRITY BMW

Famous owners

A BMW in your drive says a lot about you. Obviously you've got taste, money (if it's a new one) and you're probably very successful. But some people think that's showing off! Some celebrities don't even want to own up to the fact that they've got one in their garage! However, here's a few of the many owners who don't mind revealing why they chose a BMW.

Liverpool Captain, with over 650 appearances, leading them to League Championships as well as FA and European Cups. These days though he's probably better known as the excitable Captain of his celebrity team in 'A Question of Sport'. And when it comes to a question of cars, there's absolutely no doubt, it has to be BMWs. When the picture was taken Emlyn was running a metallic green 635 CSi. In the past he's had two 2500s, a 7 and two other 6 series. I think he quite likes them. [Autocar & Motor]

Emlyn Hughes

106

Spurs, England, West Ham, Barnet. The connection is goals and lots of them, scored by one brilliant striker. Jimmy Greaves has moved with ease from the world of soccer into television, becoming one of the most successful TV pundits and popular comedy teams with Ian St. John. He's also no mean driver, having finished 6th in the 1970 World Cup Rally in a Ford Escort. Jimmy's relationship with BMWs goes back to a 2800 saloon, virtually the forerunner of the 528i he owned when the picture was taken. [Autocar & Motor]

Jimmy Greaves

Eddy Shah

For a man as busy as Eddy Shah there's no time to lose in the competitive business world. So his BMW becomes his mobile office, the telephone keeping him in touch with developments and the car taking him safely to meetings. After owning a 735 Eddy now runs a 750i. At the time BMW (GB) made sure that he was the very first customer to receive the new model in the UK. [Sunday Times]

107

BMW Financ◄
Racing with Mobil **1**

Mobil **1** Mobil **1** Mobil **1** Mobil **1** Mobil **1**

BMW Finance

Mobil **1**

BMW Finance

Mobil **1**

Mobil **1**

BMW Finance

BMW Finance

1988 BRITISH TOURING CAR CHAMPIONSHIP Mar 27 Silverstone - Apr 1 Oulton Park - May 2 Thruxton - May 15 Donington Park - May 30 Thruxton
5 Silverstone - Jul 10 Silverstone - Jul 24 Brands Hatch - Jul 31 Snetterton - Aug 21 Brands Hatch - Aug 29 Birmingham - Sept 18 Donington Park - Oct 2 Silverst◄

On the right is DJ and television personality Mike Smith who competed in the 1988 British Touring Car Championship and acquitted himself very well, before injury forced him out of the later rounds. Mike used a road going M3 to acclimatise himself to the left-handed driving position. His partner Frank Sytner went on to win the Championship outright.

John Surtees

In 1956, Count Agusta, who owned the MV motorcycle concern, offered John Surtees a choice of motor car as a sort of prize for winning the World 500 cc motorcycle championship. He opted for a BMW 507. It was stylish and fast, appropriate transport to take him to race meetings. John still owns the car today and it is one of his most treasured possessions. (Sunday Times)

Leslie Grantham

Soap fans know him better as 'Dirty Den.' And if they can't make the distinction between an actor and the part he plays then Eastender watchers will probably be quite surprised by the car he owns. Nothing brash, nothing flash, just the stylish understated elegance of a four-door 325i. (Autocar & Motor)

Gary Wilmott

One of the funniest men on television and also one of the funniest on the roads. Now that's not a comment on his driving abilities, but the fact that he practises all his new routines, characters and impressions from the driver's seat. Apparently the quiet and relaxed surroundings of his 7 series provide the perfect rehearsal atmosphere. (Autocar & Motor)

Rob McElenea

Better known as a two-wheeled racer Rob is a works Yamaha driver. This more subtly coloured 325i doesn't draw as much attention as his previous bright red example that landed him with a month's ban. (Autocar & Motor)

Jon Lord

A heavy metal exponent, *Deep Purple's* keyboard player, with the heaviest metal that Munich currently produces, the 750i. Finished in metallic black this was the very first of the V12 7s in the UK. Jon is no stranger to BMWs having owned three others over the years. (Autocar & Motor)

Stirling Moss

Stirling looks decidedly unhappy about sharing the close confines of a British-built Isetta bubble car with several unidentified blondes. The carpet-like ride had something to do with the location being the Grosvenor House Hotel where the Brighton Bubbles were officially launched.

Spotted with a BMW

Stirling Moss

Here he is several years later when his association with the marque was renewed. However, the World Championship winning BT 52 was slightly faster than the Bubble.

Emerson Fittipaldi

Formula 1 Champion in '72 and '74. Showing incredible taste in his choice of cars, if not his choice of clothes, but they were fashionable at the time.

BMW at the movies

Robert Wagner

Film star. Seen here slumming it with a 635 outside the BMW headquarters in Munich. Actually the coupé was his runabout for his TV role as an insurance detective in the series *55 Lime Street*.

Make mein tag (Make my day)

The BMW 3.2 V8 appeared in *Here is Isar 12* an apparently popular thriller series which featured the Munich police and their faithful criminal catcher capable of 110 mph.

Other memorable appearances by BMWs on screen have included: *Moonlighting* – David Addison (Bruce Willis) and Maddie Hayes (Cybill Shepherd) share driving duties in their 635. Although on one occasion it was virtually written off in an underground car park. *Lytton's Diary* – incredibly suave Peter Bowles completes the act of a smooth newspaperman by tooling around in a 2002 cabriolet. *Crazy Like a Fox* – More American detective duos plump for a BM, this time it's a 7. Presumably so that Jack Warden can squeeze in. *Star Chamber* – Michael Douglas does a Clint Eastwood impression as an avenging judge behind the wheel of his 5

series. *Splash* – At the Disney end of Hollywood Tom Hanks finds a mermaid and takes her (Daryl Hannah) everywhere in a 528i. *Pop video* – Kylie Minogue displayed good taste in abundance when she was pictured bounding around in the back of a 3 series cabriolet for the single, *I should be so lucky*. *Auf Wiedersehen Pet* – Wayne's (Gary Holton) old 5 series may be left-hand drive and German registered, but it still pulled the birds and took him safely down the autobahn.

Facing page, top:
A BMW submarine!
Powered by a BMW marine
engine it was a scale model
of a real U-boat. It was
used in a popular feature
film. You might have seen
Das Boot at your local art
house cinema. It was
Germany's most
internationally successful film.

Paint your wagen

There's more to a racing car than simply sticking numbers on the side, or turning it into a mobile advertising billboard. Why not carefully transform it into a work of art? During the '70s BMW were just as committed to aesthetically pleasing paint schemes on their cars as to the winning of races.

Alexander Calder (1975)

Here with his poster paint shapes on a 3.0 CSL. Behind him a bunch of mobiles (which he invented) and a bunch of BMW personnel looking more pleased with the result than Calder himself, but only just.

115

Frank Stella (1976)

Mr. Stella with a scale model of his graph proposal for a 3.0 CSL Turbo. Behind him, one he prepared earlier.

Roy Lichtenstein (1977)

Here Mr. Lichtenstein prods at a scale 320i in his studio. And ...

... the real thing!

Andy Warhol (1979)

Andy adds his monicker to the bumper of an M1 he's just covered in paint. What a colourful pit stop!

The fastest art in the world in action!

The tradition has been carried on into the '80s as this 'transparent' 635 driven by Dieter Quester proves.

BMW
bits and pieces

BMW bits and pieces

Here's a series of fascinating facts, unusual observations and strange pictures. Basically, things that wouldn't fit neatly into any other part of the book.

Most luxurious and expensive BMW

These days that's probably the 750iL. However, the 735iA Special Equipment Executive Version introduced to the UK in 1984, which also ranks as the longest ever

name to be given to a BMW, was pretty plush. Buffalo hide, walnut cappings and electric everything else added up to a sumptuous package. However, the 505 limousine from '55 was equally plush if less high tech.

Fastest BMW afloat

That's right, BMW make boats too! Their marine engines have powered boats for many years, and being BMWs they're usually quite extraordinary craft. Here Dieter Quester sets the world kilometre record in 1968, covering the course at 136.106 kph.

BMW airborne

After all, that's how they started originally supplying engines for Fokkers and Heinkels. Pictured is a Junkers JU 52 with three BMW 132 engines dwarfing a 7 series.

Most expensive snow plough

Yes it's the M1 again.

The most valuable transporter full of BMWs

Here's 6 race-prepared M1s for the '79 PROCAR season. Offers over £^{1}/$_2$m for the lot might still be turned down. And wherever else will you ever get to see 6 M1s together, let alone one!

Best dressed BMWs

Spot the dummy. BMW's M style range of accessories preceded many of today's motor merchandise spin offs. M style will cover you from head to toe in tracksuits, pullovers, raincoats, jackets, shirts, scarves, towels, sunglasses, wallets, umbrellas, watches and probably cuddly toys.

Most convincing Z1 prototype

In fact, this is a partially built 501 from 1952.

Most popular police car

What a stylish way to catch baddies. A common sight in Germany and the Metropolitan Police have 5s in London too.

Ugliest

It has to be the 2000 saloon and the CS coupé. But apart from the hideous front end the rest is OK.

BMW with the most records

At the moment in the UK it has to be the M3 that was prepared by Ivan Dutton for Ed Hubbard. For the sheer hell of it these motoring enthusiasts teamed up to break a few British land speed records. However, it's a miracle that any records were broken at all because during preparations the engine developed a serious fault. The Millbrook test track had been booked for the following day and Ivan Dutton had to remove the boot lid from his 5 series and dash across country to pick up a replacement engine. The new unit was installed overnight and the next day everything went as planned.

10 Class D records! At 5 km, 5 miles, 10 km, 10 miles, 50 km, 50 miles, 100 km, 100 miles, 200 km, 200 miles and 1 hour. The highest speed recorded in this virtually standard car was 152.05 mph. (Photos courtesy of Ivan Dutton).

BMW with the most unusual record

The car in question is a 745i. The record is the European Car Top Ski-ing Record. In anyone's book, being strapped to the roof of a speeding car in fluorescent pink overalls isn't normal. But nonetheless the Aitken Building Society Group, Mobil Oils and AVA Turbo Systems got together to break a record. The car had been modified to produce 300 bhp with lowered front suspension which gives the downward attitude that rooftop skiers need. Driven by AVA Director Alan Clark with his brother Norman on top, the attempt was made at Machrihanish Air Base in Scotland because it has one of the longest runways in Britain (10,000 feet). The previous record stood at 134 mph and the BMW with help from the Clark Brothers raised that to 141.5 mph. Not only that, they succeeded in raising £3,000 for the charity Back Up which helps out the spinally injured. You can now find this BMW in the *Guinness Book of Records*. (Photo courtesy of Aitken Building Group).

Rarities

To finish off this section, here's a selection of rare BMWs and close relatives.

Car: K Wagen
Year: 1939
Designed: by Professor Kamra, hence the name 'K' Wagen, geddit??!!?
Based on: The elegant 335 chassis (see back), *but* you can't help thinking that the original body was somewhat more appropriate.
Purpose: To produce a more slippery shape for autobahn cruising.

Car: Touring Prototype
Year: 1940
Based on: 328 Roadster
Purpose: Here's what the 328 would have become if the war hadn't intervened. It's all tooled up for the Mille Miglia event, but sadly was never raced.

Car: Veritas.
Year: 1951
Numbers built: Just 80 (Touring and convertibles).
Designed by: Ernst Loof with many other ex-BMW employees. But forbidden to use the BMW name.
Based on: 328 with modified 6-cylinder, chassis and all new body
The End: BMW took over the company in 1953.

Car: 505 limousine
Year: 1955
Styled by: Giovanni Michelotti
Numbers built: 2
Specification: Intercom/Electric divide/Wood trim/119.5 inch wheelbase
Purpose: To compete with Mercedes and Rolls-Royce. It didn't.

Car: BMW Farmobil
Based on: 700 mechanics.
Other details: None.

129

Car: Elva BMW GT 160
Styled by: Trevor Fiore
Built by: Fissore in Italy
Details: Just 3 were built.
British connection: GB built
French connection: Name derived from 'Elle va' translated: She goes . . .

Car: BMW Glas 3000 V8
Styled by: Frua
Nickname: Glaserati
Performance: The Glas V8 produced 160 bhp and could exceed 120 mph.
Numbers built: Sources vary, somewhere between 300 and 400.
Killed off: 1968, to make production room for the 2500 saloon and so that it didn't compete with the 2800CS.

Car: 2002 in disguise.
Styled by: Frua of Italy.
First shown: Frankfurt Show 1969
Details: Only one example was built.

Car: Turbo
Year: 1972
Styled by: Paul Bracq
Styling features: Gull wing doors, fibreglass body.
Mechanical features: Used 2002tii's engine, but turbo charged.
Purpose: Experimental safety vehicle with energy-absorbing bumpers, side impact bars, roll bar, radar warning device to warn driver that car in front too close.
Numbers built: 2
Turned into: The M1

Car: M3 Evolution
Year: 1988
Numbers: 500 (40 to GB)
Mechanical features: 10% increase in power over 'ordinary' M3 to 220 bhp raising top speed to 152 mph and returning a 0–62 mph time of 6.7 seconds.

Purpose: Built for homologation purposes so that BMW could maintain their dominance on the race track.
Sum up: Latest in a long line of limited edition BMW classics. You could go a whole lifetime without ever seeing one!

Previous page:

From computers to the test track – that's how quickly new models are being developed by BMW. Here, something new is being put through its damp paces on the Munich test track.

BMW Technik

It took just two years for BMW's other company within a company, Technik, to design, develop and build the Z1. This gives us many clear pointers for the future as it demonstrates the company's ability to offer limited edition models. These cars also function as a test bed for advanced technical features, which will eventually be incorporated into the normal production models.

Inside information

1: A coupé version of the Z1 is being developed and will probably be called the Z2.

Inside information

2: A British firm is planning to import the cars and make them street legal for our roads.

Inside information

3: A limited edition successor to the M1 is being planned. M2?

BMW motorsport

There are ambitious plans for BMW's racing programme. The '80s have been very successful, particularly the 3 series whose involvement in saloon racing and rallying is likely to increase.

Inside information

1: Turbo versions of the M3 and possibly M5, for racing purposes only.

Inside information

2: BMW's return to Formula 1. The M3's highly developed four-cylinder and the new V12 make their re-entry into the class very likely.

M3s still going to form the backbone of any racing effort. BMW also have an impressive roster of drivers to choose from.

British connection

The environment: Lead is harmful to both the environment and the population and any moves to reduce that level of pollution have to be applauded. Already, production BMWs can be simply converted to run on unleaded fuel.

The fuel: As lead is an octane booster, its removal usually results in a loss of power.

The racetrack: Using unleaded fuel on the racetrack would seem to be the quickest way to lose. However, it is possible to make up that octane deficiency which Fina have done with tertiary amyl methyl ether unit at their refineries.

The first: When Fina mated their fuel with the M3 they formed the perfect winning partnership and also the first sports car to run on unleaded petrol.

The success: In their first season in 1988 the Fina team won the British Production Car Championship. The racing of tomorrow is already taking place today.

Profile Dr Wolfgang Reitzle

1976: Joined as production technology expert and eventually became head of technical central planning.

1987: Appointed Director of Research & Development.

Dr. Reitzle is currently presiding over one of the most exciting and active periods in BMW's history with the new 5 and 7 series cars recently launched, the Z1 and all-new 3 and 6(8) series cars almost in production.

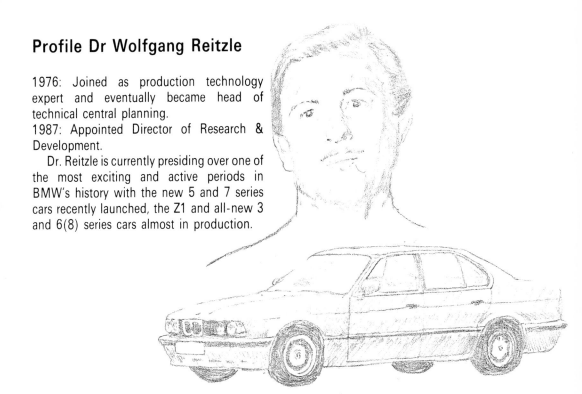

Inside information

1: The R&D team are developing an active suspension system, similar to that used in Formula 1 racing.

Inside information

2: R&D will produce multi-valve cylinder heads to boost the performance of the 4- and 12-cylinder engines.

BMW: Next century or next year?

What will future BMWs look like? No one really knows except the designers themselves. However, some interesting proposals have been put together in the last few years to show that BMW are always thinking ahead.

A 5-door saloon, next century's 5 series? The emphasis is on optimum visibility and a practical hatchback, or touring shape.

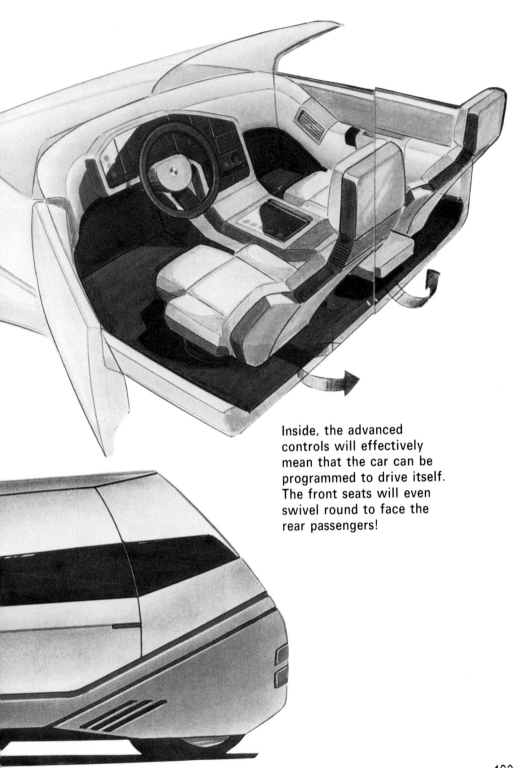

Inside, the advanced
controls will effectively
mean that the car can be
programmed to drive itself.
The front seats will even
swivel round to face the
rear passengers!

Known as the
mono-swinger this was
conceived before the
infamous Sinclair C5.
However, this is intended as
a high performance bath
chair with a join in the
middle to provide a smooth
ride.

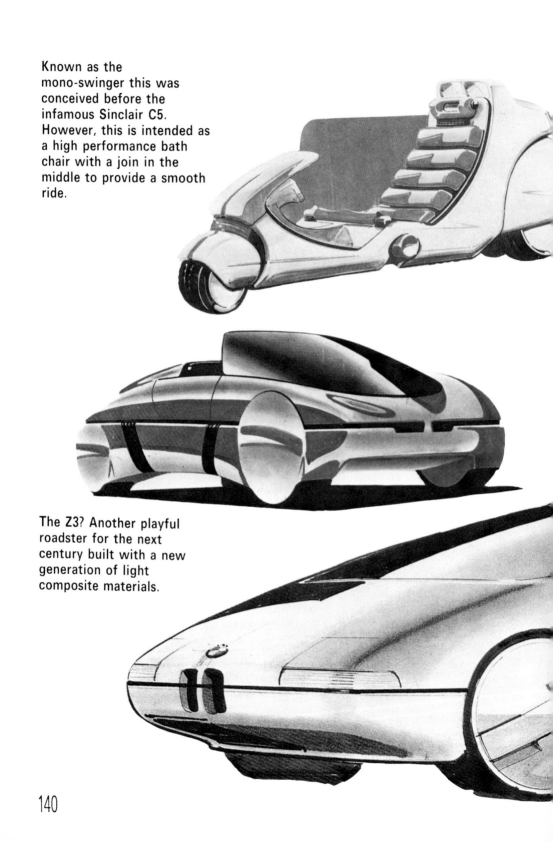

The Z3? Another playful
roadster for the next
century built with a new
generation of light
composite materials.

Why didn't anyone think of it before? A caravan and car integrated as one, although they could both be used separately. A BMW caravan! Why not?

9 Series Coupé? Has the Z1's sliding doors as well as a rear door for added practicality.

Alternative power

BMW are as aware as any other manufacturer that the earth's resources are limited and have been working on alternative ways of powering their cars for the future.

Hydrogen: BMW also have a 745i converted to run on hydrogen. But this fuel has to be kept cool – minus 253 degrees centigrade!! Top speed also drops from 132 to 124 mph.

The high energy battery which is currently being used in an experimental 325 needs to be kept hot! 300 degrees centrigrade! So it is mounted in a giant vacuum flask. A 60 mph top speed and 50 mile operating range is envisaged. Introduction of battery BMs could be very close, within the next ten years. Here's what the electric car might look like.

Conclusion

Next century's BMW may be battery powered, aerodynamically perfect and of course very fast. But that's speculation. What we can be sure of though is whatever the eventual shape, or power unit at the front, there's got to be a kidney grille!

Owners' & enthusiasts' clubs

If you're fanatical about BMWs and want to know more about them, help is at hand. In fact there are thousands of other enthusiasts all over the country who feel exactly the same way as you and they are all members of the many specialist BMW clubs. You don't even have to be a BMW owner, just absolutely nutty about the cars and everything that goes with them. Imagine whole weekends, looking around, talking about and arguing over BMWs. Newsletters that keep you up to date with BMW activities, as well as access to rare parts special insurance schemes and discounts.

So here's a brief summary of the specialist clubs which cater for BMWs. It's up to you to decide which club is right for your needs. Simply write to them and they will without obligation send you all the information that you need.

BMW DRIVERS CLUB
100% INDEPENDENT OF FACTORY & DEALERS

This club was formed in October 1979. All post-war BMWs are eligible, and although pre-1939 models are welcome, no technical back-up can be provided for them.

Members can obtain parts at a significant discount. There are a number of competitive insurance schemes. Technical advice by phone or letter is provided free of charge. And a list of BMW specialists means that work is carried out cost-effectively to the highest possible standard. There's also a club magazine and regular bulletins to keep members fully up to date.

A full programme of national and local events includes track tests, talks and rallies.

Contact:

BMW Drivers Club,
PO Box 8,
Dereham,
Norfolk.

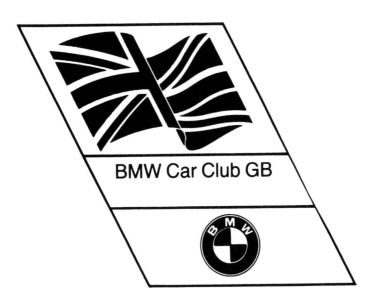

BMW Car Club GB

Open to all owners and enthusiasts of BMW cars, this club has an extensive regional network that covers almost all of the country.

A full colour magazine appears three times a year, along with regular newsletters to keep members informed of forthcoming events and activities. These include visits to Munich, the GB headquarters in Bracknell, concours, driving tests and dinner dances. There are also affiliations with international BMW clubs and events are often held in conjunction with those bodies.

Other services include technical advice, club clothing, reprinting of handbooks and motor insurance.

Contact:

BMW Car Club
558 London Road,
Isleworth,
Middlesex TW7 4EP.

ISETTA OWNERS CLUB
of
GREAT BRITAIN

Formed in 1978 the club caters for the original Italian Isetta cars, but also all the BMW variants, 250, 300 and 600, as well as the 700.

Most importantly the club has access to a large range of parts and if the demand is there, will undertake the re-manufacture of certain spares. They even run a used parts service. Photostats of original workshop manuals are also available. Valuable technical advice is provided by the club.

A newsletter keep members fully informed of the many national and local events. It also contains a 'bubble mart' classified ad section.

A register attempts to keep tabs on all the surviving three- and four-wheeled examples that remain in the country.

Contact:

Brian Orris
Membership Secretary,
Isetta Owners Club,
30 Durham Road,
Sidcup,
Kent DA14 6LH.

This is not a complete directory of every BMW specialist but it should include at least one or two companies which may be able to help you find that elusive part, finish that attempted restoration and perhaps make it move just a little more quickly.

Inclusion in this section does not necessarily imply recommendation of the companies concerned as neither author, nor publisher will be aware of managerial changes or policy after publication.

B & B Components
1A Queen Anne Road,
Maidstone,
Kent.
0622 677662/685308
Parts

BM Sport – BMW Racing
The Forge,
Newchurch,
Romney Marsh,
Kent TN29 0DL.
0303 874433
Race prep, parts restoration.

Heathrow BMW Ltd
Unit 7,
Maple Industrial Estate,
Feltham,
Middlesex TW13 7AW
01 884 1885/7
Parts

Jaymic Ltd
Norwich Road,
Cromer,
Norfolk NR27 0HF
0263 511710
Parts Restoration 2002

Banbury Autobahn
Unit 5 Thorpe Way,
Banbury,
Oxon OX16 8SP,
0295 61196
Parts Restoration

Corry Exclusively BMW
Lower Road Garage,
62 Lower Road,
South Harrow,
Middlesex HA2 0DH.
Parts Recon.

146

Griffin Motorsport Ltd
Bagbury Park, The Street,
Lydiard Millicent,
Swindon,
Wiltshire, SN5 9LU
(0793) 771802
Griffin Conversions

Alan Cowland Spares
Finedon Sidings Trading Estate,
Station Road,
Finedon,
Northants NN9 5NY.
(05360) 723587/722438
New & Used Parts.

Mark Smith
Alrewas,
Burton-on-Trent,
Staffs.
(02830) 790786
Parts/Restoration

Birds Garage
31-33 Station Road,
Gerrards Cross,
Bucks
(07530) 888321
Hartge Conversions

Sytner
165 Huntingdon Street,
Nottingham NG1 3NH
(0602) 582831
Alpina conversions

Forge Garage
Sandy Lane
Crawley Down,
West Sussex RH10 4HS
0342 716243
Parts Restoration

Linwar Motors
40 Virginia Street,
Southport PR8 6RU
0704 40047
Parts Restoration

DPR Forced Induction Systems Ltd
Water Coombe Lane,
Lynx West Trading Estate,
Yeovil BA22 9JJ
0935 32177
Supercharging

Classic & Thoroughbred Spares
The Packhouse,
North Perrott Fruit Farm,
Crewkerne,
Somerset TA18 7SS
0460 76663
Parts & Restoration

BMV
Unit 1, Prospect Mills,
Thornton Road,
Bradford,
0274 834078
Parts

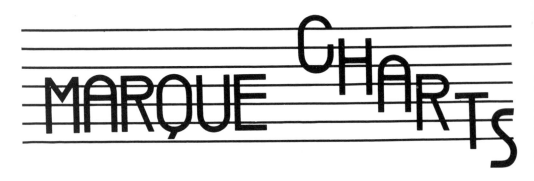

MARQUE CHARTS

Now if you wondered what model replaced which and when, these BMW Marque Charts should help. They could even settle an argument with a fellow BMW fanatic. On second thoughts though, they might even start several nasty incidents if my research is wrong.

I've put in as much detail as possible without bogging you down with every single version or derivative. I've also excluded some of the European models that didn't make it over here.

Make sure you take notes because questions may be asked later during the Trivia Test.

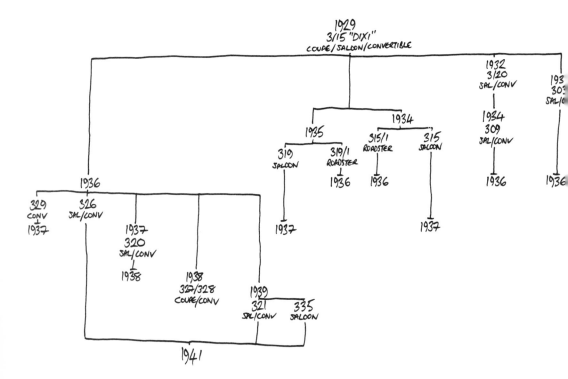

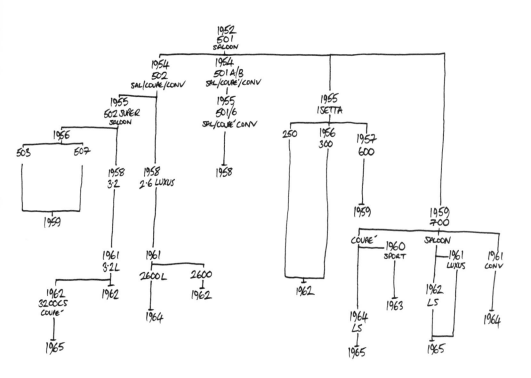

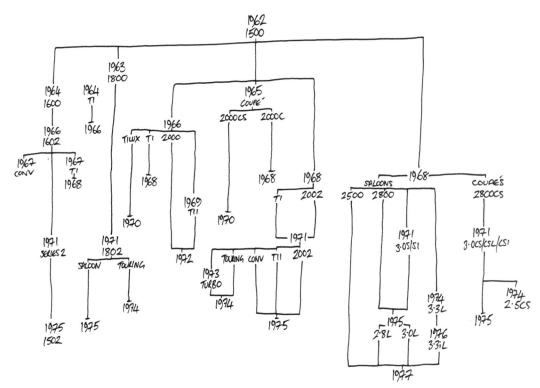

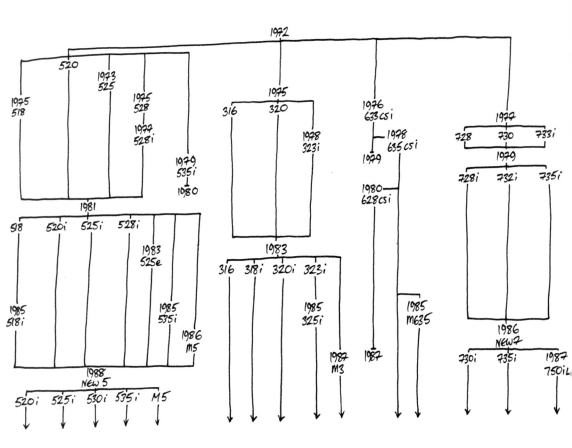

BMW TRIVIA QUIZ

Here it is, the moment you've been waiting for – the end of the book. However, it isn't quite over yet. Why not pit your wits against Professor Gustav Foresight who came up with this brain-tickling quiz. All the teasers contained here are based on the information within the BMW Driver's Book, so there are no excuses.

1. True or false? (i) The BMW roundel is based on a 14th century Bavarian coat of arms. (ii) Albrecht von Goertz, designer of the 503 and 507, built hot rods in America. (iii) People often mistake 1500 saloons for Ladas.

2.

Identify these cabriolets.

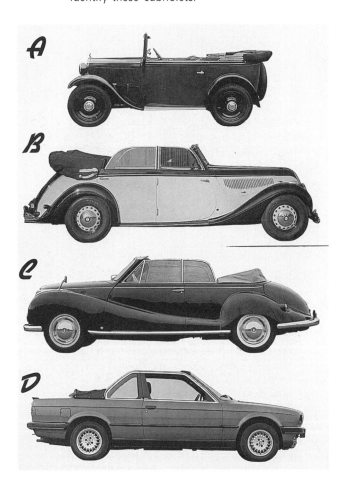

o? What? When?

4. Who did the paint job on this car? And name three other artists who've been let loose on BM bodywork.

5. BMW Algebra.

 −  ÷

 +

= ?

6. Identify these BMW Drivers

(i)   (ii)   (iii)

7.
The famous kidney grille hasn't appeared on some models. Which ones?

8.

Across
1. It could burst. (6)
2. Motorway cruiser. (2)
3. Powerful Dozen. (3)
4. ****** Beat. (6)
5. Composed celebrity. (6)

Down
1. Home town. (6)
2. Abbreviated Dept. (2)
3. See 1 down, but wider. (7)
4. Loaded BM. (2)
5. Luxurious and lucky. (5)

9. What's the connection between these two?

10. What comes next?

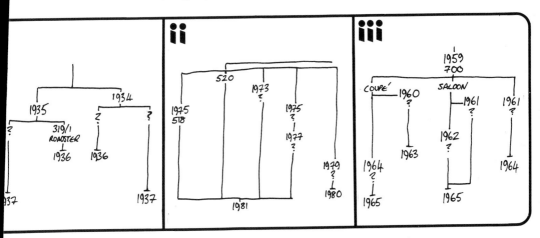

(now turn page for ✓ or ✗)

THE SOLUTIONS

How to score. One mark for each correct answer which includes a mark for each sub-question and every crossword line you solve.

1. (i) False. (ii) True. (iii) True.
2. (a) 3/20 (b) 335 (c) 501/3 (d) 323i Baur.
3. Nelson Piquet. Brabham BMW BT 52. 1983 The Championship season.
4. Frank Stella. The others are Alexander Calder, Roy Lichtenstein, Andy Warhol.
5. $2800 - 730 \div 507 + 502 = 506.083$.
6. (i) John Surtees.
   (ii) Emerson Fittipaldi.
   (iii) Robert Wagner.
7. 3/15. 3/20. Isetta. 700. 600. BMW Glas.

8.

9. This splendid 24 valve engine.

156

10. (i)

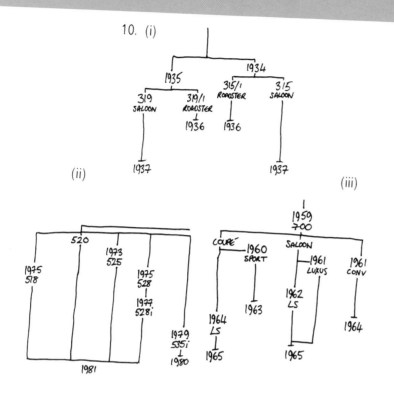

(ii)   (iii)

How did you score and what does it all mean?

0 – 15 Seek medical attention. You really can do a lot better than this. Back to page one.

15 – 30 Congratulations, you're not as stupid as you look. A respectable score, but you're certainly no Einstein. Make sure you take notes next time you thumb through the BMW Driver's Book.

30–40 Cheat. If not, your head is likely to have trouble negotiating doorways. Re-read the book, but don't pay too much attention this time.

STOP PRESS

include a convertible, four-wheel steering and an infra-red, poor visibility driving aid. There will also be smaller engined versions, the 830i and 835i in the early '90s. Development of 32 valve V8 units are also rumoured and even a 5.4 litre 40 valve V12 to power an M8!!!

750i

A shortened sports chassis makes the top of the range BMW one of the most exciting luxury saloons in the world. Combining power with refinement the 300 bhp five-litre engine accelerates the car from zero to 62 mph in just 7.4 seconds and on to an electronically limited speed of 155 mph. Apart from the shorter wheelbase the only

It's often difficult to keep up with the pace of change in the motor industry and this book is no exception. Between completion and publication there have been new models, products and developments. Here's a selection of the most important events that give valuable pointers to the future of BMW which we were just able to squeeze in.

850i

Replacing the 13 year old 6 Series, deliveries of the new car will begin in spring 1990 although it may not reach the UK until the end of that year. Powered by the mighty V12, top speed will be equivalent to the existing 750i, but the acceleration should be significantly better because of the optional six-speed gearbox. Future developments should

other distinguishing feature of this saloon is the inclusion of cross-spoke alloys with extra wide 240/50 ZR 415 Michelin TRX tyres and electrically-operated sports seats.

318i Touring

BMW extend the range and the appeal of the Touring models by installing the 115 bhp, 1800 cc M40 unit, their best selling engine during 1988. This now represents the 24th model in the entire 3-series range which goes on getting longer and more successful all the time.

At the time of going to press, new 3 series models were expected by the end of 1990, although they wouldn't go on sale until the following year. The Touring will be dropped in favour of a 5 series estate. The existing M3 and cabriolet will continue into the early '90s. The design of the new cars will be much more aerodynamic, although they will be based on the current model's chassis.

E1

If you're after an indication of how next century's BMW will look, this is it. The E1 is a styling exercise that anticipates new materials which would allow such a radical concept to succeed. Nice to see that the kidney grille has made it into the 2000s.

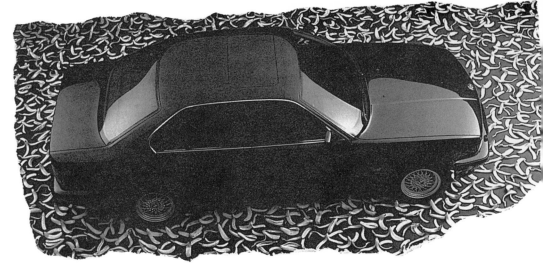

Advertising

There have, of course, been many more original BMW ads recently. One of the most eye catching featured this 5 series surrounded by 1500 banana skins. The point was to highlight the advantages of BMW's ASC (anti-slip acceleration system). Apparently, the bananas were hand peeled then dipped in wax to preserve them so that they did not discolour under the hot studio lights. Incidentally, London Zoo were on the receiving end of the tasty middle bits.

As another April 1st came and went, BMW's prankery was up to the usual incredibly high standard. Without going into too much detail, this ad was all about the new DWS (Driver's Weight Sensor) system. Basically, if you don't tally with the weight as recorded by the on-board computer, off goes the alarm, alerting all walkie-talkie carrying PCs in the area. Of course the reply coupon invited you to contact Hugh Phelfrett.

BEFORE A BMW WILL STA
IT WEIGHS UP WHO'S DRIV

First BMW brought you ABS, for safer braking in the wet.

Then came ASC, to help to counter wheelspin during acceleration.

Today, they can unveil DWS: probably the most significant advance in anti-theft technology to occur in recent years.

DWS stands for Driver's Weight Sensor.

A unique system that compares the driver's weight with a pre-programmed value stored in the sensor's computer memory.

If the two readings do not match, the car simply refuses to start.

Clearly, this represents a whole new level of anti-theft sophistication.

But one that has only been made possible thanks to recent advances in space satellite PHAT technology.

This remarkable new material – Poly Halide Anodal Tritium – exhibits a highly predictable change in electrical conductivity according to the pressure exerted upon it.

By harnessing these properties, BMW's engineers have devised a wafer-thin pressure pad that, when incorporated into the driver's seat, can electronically assess the occupant's weight to within 10 grams accuracy.

Such is the system's intelligence, it will take account of bodyweight variations that occur according to the time of day, or even the time of year.

This it achieves by interlocking with the car's on-board 365 day digital clock.

Accurate allowances can then be made for weight increases that may be expected immediately after meal times, and those that are caused by heavy multi-layered clothing during the winter months.

Despite its space age technology, the operation of DWS is simplicity itself.

On entering the car, the driver inserts the ignition key, at which point the words 'Code Enter' flash up on the dashboard LED display. Up to five of these codes may be stored for five different drivers.

The driver now enters his personal code on the key pad and his weight appears on the lightup display, expressed in either pounds or kilos.

(Lady drivers who would prefer this visible display switched off should consult their BMW dealer, who will carry out the small necessary adjustment free of charge.)

The sensor weight reading is then compared to the programmed weight in the memory, and provided this falls to within ±5%, the car will start normally.

If, however, the figure exceeds these tolerances, then a discreet gong sounds, and the entire ignition system is shut down.

Should persistent attempts be made to restart the car, an alarm system is triggered, and the headlights flash alternately until the unauthorised person vacates the seat and re-closes the door.

At the same time a pre-recorded message is transmitted on the standard police radio frequency, notifying all walkie-talkie equipped police officers within 350 metres of the car's registration number.

If you'd like to know whether the Driver's Weight Sensor anti-theft system can be fitted to your car, contact your local BMW dealer, or post off the coupon below.

Send to: Hugh Phelfrett, BMW Information Service, PO Box 46, Hounslow, Middlesex TW4 6NF. Please send me more details of the BMW Driver's Weight Sensor System. My weight is.

☐ Under 10 stone ☐ 10-12 stone ☐ None of your business

First Name & Title

Surname

Address

Post Code

Present Car & Year

THE ULTIMATE DRIVING MACHINE